TULLIAN TCHIVIDJIAN

CARNAGE & Grace

Confessions of an *Adulterous* Heart

LUCIDBOOKS

Carnage & Grace
Confessions of an Adulterous Heart

Copyright © 2024 by Tullian Tchividjian

Published by Lucid Books in Houston, TX
www.LucidBooks.com

Scripture quotations marked (ASV) are taken from the American Standard Version (ASV): American Standard Version, public domain.

Scripture quotations marked Book of Common Prayer are from the Episcopal Church. The Book of Common Prayer and Administration of the Sacraments and Other Rites and Ceremonies of the Church: Together with the Psalter or Psalms of David According to the Use of the Episcopal Church: Seabury Press, 1979.

Scripture quotations marked (ESV) are taken from the ESV® Bible (The Holy Bible, English Standard Version®), copyright © 2001 by Crossway, a publishing ministry of Good News Publishers. Used by permission. All rights reserved.

Scripture quotations marked (MSG) are taken from THE MESSAGE, copyright © 1993, 2002, 2018 by Eugene H. Peterson. Used by permission of NavPress. All rights reserved. Represented by Tyndale House Publishers, Inc.

Scripture quotations marked (NIV) are taken from the Holy Bible, New International Version®, NIV®. Copyright ©1973, 1978, 1984, 2011 by Biblica, Inc.™ Used by permission of Zondervan. All rights reserved worldwide. www.zondervan.com The "NIV" and "New International Version" are trademarks registered in the United States Patent and Trademark Office by Biblica, Inc.™

Scripture quotations marked (NRSV) are taken from the New Revised Standard Version Bible, copyright 1989, Division of Christian Education of the National Council of the Churches of Christ in the United States of America. Used by permission. All rights reserved."

ISBN: 978-1-63296-638-4 (Paperback)
ISBN: 978-1-63296-637-7 (Hardback)
eISBN: 978-1-63296-690-2

Special Sales: Most Lucid Books titles are available in special quantity discounts. Custom imprinting or excerpting can also be done to fit special needs. Contact Lucid Books at Info@LucidBooks.com

To my three adult children—Gabe, Nate, and Genna:

I pray that my failures—past, present, and future—teach you more about God's grace than any of my successes ever could. I love you three so, so much.

"Call me sleepless from the road,
when the rivers going down,
when the skies are laying low,
and shadows follow you wherever you go . . .
I will leave a light on."

—Le Youth x Lane 8

And to Stacie—what can I say?

You're living proof to me that God gives us his best when we're at our worst.

"And here with you,
I'm not alone,
I found a place to call my own . . ."

—Lane 8

CONTENTS

ACKNOWLEDGMENTS
NOTES
ABOUT THE AUTHOR

THE LAUGHING HEART

Your life is your life
Don't let it be clubbed into dank submission.
Be on the watch.
There are ways out.
There is a light somewhere.
It may not be much light but
It beats the darkness.
Be on the watch.
The gods will offer you chances.
Know them.
Take them.
You can't beat death but
You can beat death in life, sometimes.
And the more often you learn to do it,
The more light there will be.
Your life is your life.
Know it while you have it.
You are marvelous
The gods wait to delight
In you.

—Charles Bukowski

Prologue
CARNAGE & GRACE

> We all have regrets and most of us know that those regrets, as excruciating as they can be, are the things that help us lead improved lives. Or, rather, there are certain regrets that, as they emerge, can accompany us on the incremental bettering of our lives. Regrets are forever floating to the surface . . . They require our attention. You have to do something with them. One way is to seek forgiveness by making what might be called living amends, by using whatever gifts you may have in order to help rehabilitate the world.
>
> —Nick Cave and Sean O'Hagan, *Faith, Hope and Carnage*

For a white, middle-aged, straight, well-known but disgraced male minister to publish a memoir right now makes no sense. None at all. The air's too charged, the ice too thin. But "screw it, I'll go first." That's a phrase from my friend Nadia Bolz-Weber. I'll give some context to that phrase later in the book, but my gut tells me you get it already. It's simple and direct and powerful.

The title of this memoir is *Carnage & Grace*. You're familiar with the word *grace*, it's almost worn threadbare in our current culture, applied to everything from an obligatory brief "thank you" before meals to the mind-bendingly angelic way Simone Biles tumbles through the air to the transcendent way DJ *Lane 8* takes listeners on a melodic journey through their emotions. And while I agree with all of those uses, I've learned of a grace that's got some teeth to it, a gritty grace that shines brightest when contrasted with the darkness of bloody slaughter and injury that results from struggle and battle and war—in a word, *carnage*. There's a lot of carnage in the pages that follow. An excruciating amount. And I've regrets. As the subtitle clearly states, these are "confessions of an adulterous heart."

But I wanted to do something with those regrets, hopefully something that matters, something that might be helpful, redemptive even—for me, yes, but also possibly for you. I've learned that our pains, whether self-induced or caused by others or both, can be redeeming if they're harnessed to help others find healing. In her final novel, *Villette*, Charlotte Brontë wrote, "I doubt if I have made the best use of all my calamities."[1] So, this is my attempt to put my regrets to good use. Because although I wasn't for a long time, I'm getting better. And let me be crystal clear, by "getting better," in no way do I mean I'm becoming a "better person," whatever the hell that even means. What I mean is that there has been, and continues to be, real healing—there's more light in my life, more peace, more laughter. That's why I included the poem by Charles Bukowski (yes, definitely no angel) in this Prologue. I want to share with you my story of crashing and burning—the carnage—and learning through it all to trust more and more that nothing else in this inescapably hard life matters as much as our belovedness, and how in the end that leaves us so very free, at times bordering on giddy. This telling of my story is simply one piece of my ongoing daily work of making a "living amends" for the *carnage* I've caused, something I can only do because of *grace*.

Our adulterous hearts (and we've all got one) will break our own hearts and the hearts of those we love. Those broken hearts thankfully can be mended with time and attention and God's mercy. But those two movements, almost like inhaling and exhaling, will continue throughout our time on this earth—break then mend, break then mend. But in all that breaking, there's a thread that runs through our lives if we've the guts to see it—that is the thread of a laughing heart—one that's been forgiven again and again and again.

I'm not sure what all heaven's going to be like, but I firmly believe it'll be a place filled with laughter—that deep belly-roaring, utterly humbling hilarity of joy like the prodigal son experienced when his father saw him from a long way off and started running, scooped him up, and said with a boisterous mirth-filled heart, "I'm so glad you're home!"

> There was some one thing that was too great for God to show us when He walked upon our earth; and I have sometimes fancied that it was His mirth.
>
> —G. K. Chesterton, *Orthodoxy*

Oh, are Nadia Bolz-Weber and Charles Bukowski the kind of company I keep? Yes, for they're the kind of company I am.

Two other things you need to know. First, this is a memoir. Biography is the narrative of a life, the whole shooting match, birth to death and maybe even beyond in some strange cases. Memoir, on the other hand, is a snapshot of a specific time or season in a life. This is a memoir—a *click* of a specific time in my life when I got lost, and then got found. And while facts are vital to a memoir, it is the story of a season as best as the author remembers it—*memoir*, from the French *memoire* or "memory." So, while it is impossible to say *everything* that was true during that season, everything you're about to read *is* true.

Second, the word *adulterous*. For a long time, I defined that word and its variations as most people do: "sex between a married person and a person who is not his or her spouse." Very specific, literal with a heavy emphasis on the sex. My definition now, and as I'm using it in this memoir, is much broader. Yes, it does cover that very specific scenario, of which I am guilty. But an adulterous heart is much more than that, a lot more than that. Far from letting me off some hook, I believe it hangs us all on one. But I'll go first.

Part 1

THE ADULTEROUS HEART

Chapter 1
GOD'S THERE

Don't approach your history as something to be shaken for its cautionary fruit. Tell your stories, and your story will be revealed. Don't be afraid of appearing angry, small-minded, obtuse, mean, immoral, amoral, calculating, or anything else. Take no care for your dignity. Those were hard things for me to come by, and I offer them to you for what they may be worth.

—Note from Tobias Wolff to Mary Karr

When it comes to writing memoir, there are a few people who rise to the top, and one in particular who almost singlehandedly revived the genre—Mary Karr. Now, you're either drawn to Karr's "black-belt sinner" honesty or you're not; there's rarely anyone on the fence. This is how the chapter titled "God Shopping" begins in her 2009 memoir *Lit*:

> If you'd told me even a year before I started taking
> Dev to church regular that I'd wind up whispering my
> sins in the confessional or on my knees saying the rosary,

I would've laughed myself cockeyed. More likely pastime? Pole dancer. International spy. Drug mule. Assassin.

One Sunday I'm eating a bagel with a smear and reading the paper when Dev, age eight, intensely blue-eyed in his Power Ranger pajamas, announces he wants to go to church.

I barely look up. Despite my prayer life, organized religion still strikes me as bogus. Though Mother had pored over sacred texts of every kind, she was—as I've said before—no more able to commit to faith than to a husband. She quoted Marx calling religion the opiate of the masses. So I'm suspect of hierarchies.

Idly asking Dev why he wants to go to church, I'm confident that no sentence he utters will rouse me from my Sunday loll. But he says: *to see if God's there.*[2]

In Karr's book *The Art of Memoir*, she brings that same honesty to describing both the agony and the ecstasy of writing a memoir: "But nobody I know who's written a great one described it as anything less than a major-league shit-eating contest."[3]

Nobody can accuse Karr of using boring language. A "major-league shit-eating contest"? That sounds awful, but I'll play. I'm going to tell you about myself in these pages, in other words some of my story, in still another word—*memoir*. I'm going to tell you some things that may make you uncomfortable. They make me uncomfortable still. But when it comes to the journey for a memoirist, or any human for that matter, telling the truth is where it all begins or at least it should. Yet I also want to tell my story in such a way that while telling you about me, I also tell you a little, if not a lot, about God. You might react to that by accusing me of being a name-dropper, playing the God-card, diluting the wrong in my story with God's right, what Flannery O'Connor called, "propaganda on the side of the angels."[4] You could accuse me of that, but I can't write my story minus the central thread, that of God and his mercy. It's simply impossible. See, sorta like Karr's son Dev, I went to my story to see if God's there.

Guess what? God is.

The publishers will probably tag this book as a "memoir with a message," which sounds irritatingly cliché to me. But that truly is my desire—that at the conclusion of this book you'd still feel uncomfortable, if not outright uneasy, about human beings like me but ultimately hopeful when it comes to God.

My friend David Zahl uses a phrase (coined by his father, Paul Zahl) to describe that uneasy feeling about humans (which is also the title of one of David's books): "low anthropology." What David's talking about is essentially a realistic view of humanity, one that confesses—we're all broken. To live with that understanding is liberating and life-giving, and it can lead to a consolation. Alain de Botton writes, "Despite the upbeat tone of society in general, there is solace in the discovery that everyone else is . . . as bewildered and regretful as we are."[5]

A major-league shit-eating contest that drops you finally in a place of *solace* when it comes to who humans are and who God is?

Yes, memoir with a message.

PICKING UP WHERE I LEFT OFF

> In fact, the older I get, the more I realize how much my life is one long testament to this abiding truth. I'm not overstating things when I say that discovering the message of God's one-way love in all its radical glory has saved my marriage, my relationship with my kids, and my ministry. So this is not an abstract subject to me. One-way love is my lifeblood.
>
> —Tullian Tchividjian, *One Way Love*

Those words of mine were published back in 2012 which, dear God, seems like a lifetime ago. I still stand by those words, but to say things got complicated after that is a gross understatement. I really had no idea. No, God's grace was not entirely abstract, but in that other, visceral sense, yes it was. You see, grace doesn't really prevail until we run out of steam, and I hadn't arrived at the place where I was out of aces. I had yet to truly thirst for grace like that psalmic deer panting for water. I had not come to the end of me, with nothing else to hold on to, no one and nowhere else to turn. I really had no idea.

THE TERRIBLE, HORRIBLE, NO GOOD, VERY BAD YEAR

Used to be . . .

There's a certain amount of longing in that phrase, isn't there? It's almost always said with a sigh. Those words immediately set up a past-tense frame of mind—some things used to be a certain way for a period of time or a season, but they're not that way now; things changed. I know this phrase well.

I used to be what some would call an influential Christian leader, following in the footsteps of my famous grandfather, Billy Graham.

That's right, Billy Graham. I used to lead a large, famous church in my hometown of Fort Lauderdale—Coral Ridge Presbyterian Church. I used to write a book a year, and they used to be award-winning bestsellers. I used to travel extensively across the country to do book tours; to speak at conferences, churches, universities, and various events. I used to be on TV every week around the globe and on the radio every day. I used to be a popular guy, a widely sought-after guy, a "successful" guy. I used to have the world by the tail, as they say. I used to have it all, and then some. In a word, I used to be a winner and, man, it felt good.

Used to be.

But then things changed. *Used to be* imploded, unraveled, and life as I knew it came crashing down. My sins caught up with me; they always do. That was the beginning of the learning years—minutes and hours and days and weeks and months of learning what it means to lose.

I used to consider two things to be secure forever and ever amen: my twenty-one-year marriage and my role as a pastor. In 2015, I lost both. I cheated on my first wife and got caught. And because of my public persona, I lost both my marriage and my ministry (and everything else) in a very public way. If you pressed me for a reason behind it all, I'd have to point to that haunting phrase in Jimmy Buffett's "Margaritaville"—*my own damn fault.*

But loss never happens in a vacuum. Those two monumental losses were the dominoes that tipped a thousand others. The loss of peace and security on my kids' faces, the loss of close friendships, the loss of purpose, the loss of public (and private) credibility, the loss of influence, the loss of confidence in God's friendship, the loss of financial stability, the loss of hope, the loss of joy, the loss of opportunity, the loss of life as I used to know it, the loss of life as I used to *love* it.

In addition to being the cause of my own losses, I caused loss in many other people's lives as well. First and foremost, I caused loss in the lives of those who depended on me as a husband, a father, and a spiritual leader who would love and protect them. I violated their trust, betrayed their confidence, and injured their hearts. I devastated them. And even though that happened years ago, the consequences remain. There isn't a day that goes by when I am not reminded in some way of what I did.

I could give you dozens of examples, but here's one seemingly small example of the further collateral damage. I was in a Barnes & Noble in 2016 when I happened to pick up a book published before my 2015 crash; it had been written by a young author whom I'd never met face-to-face. He'd reached out to me after he finished his manuscript to tell me he looked up to me and how my books and messages had greatly impacted him. He told me this would be his first book, and he'd be honored if I'd read it and possibly write an endorsement. I agreed to do it. And here I was, only a few years later, staring at my name on the back cover of his book. In that moment, I was overcome with grief. He had thought my name and words would help give his book credibility, because at the time I wrote the blurb, my credibility was through the roof. But there it was, my name, now an unmistakable scarlet letter on his hard work. I felt sick.

No, not a day goes by . . . *my own damn fault.*

And while I've learned about loss, it's also something more, a more accurate word. I've learned about death.

I was not just devastated, or hurt, or ill-used, or broken; I was dead. Unless you have been through such an experience, you may find this overblown; but my life, as I had known it, was over, gone, kaput.

—Robert Farrar Capon, *The Romance of the Word*

In the years following that death, I've met a lot of people like me. People who live with guilt and shame and regret and sadness because of what they did or didn't do. People who would do anything to go back in time and make different choices but are presently plagued by the realization that they can't. People who live in fear that they will never hope again. People who have lost everything and wonder whether they will ever enjoy life like they used to. People who battle suicidal thoughts because they'll never outrun or outlive the consequences of their bad decisions and the people they have hurt. People who endure the painful, inescapable void of broken relationships. People who struggle with believing that anybody (even God) could love them because they have done so many bad, destructive, and hurtful things. I've met a lot of people like that, people who used to be alive but now walk around dead. People who used to be found, but then got lost. As Don Henley penned in his haunting "New York Minute": "But men get lost sometimes as years unfurl."

WHAT I DIDN'T KNOW THEN

In a 1975 issue of *Playboy* magazine, Muhammad Ali said, "The man who views the world at fifty the same as he did at twenty has wasted thirty years of his life." I was wild and lost at twenty, but by the time I was thirty, I believed I could change the world. Seriously, I believed that. I mean, c'mon, who doesn't? In your thirties, you're usually at the height of your powers. But then, at fifty? Well, now I know better. I have learned that I cannot change much of anything, to say nothing of changing the world.

Try as I might, I have not been able to manufacture outcomes the way I thought I could, either in my own life or other people's. Shattered dreams, relational tension, the loss of friendships, divorce, failure, rebellious teenagers, the death of loved ones, remaining bad habits— the list is long. But live long enough, lose enough, suffer enough, and the idealism of youth fades, leaving behind the reality of life in a broken world as a broken person. Life has had a way of proving to me that I'm not on the constantly-moving-forward escalator of progress I thought I was on when I was thirty. You could call it the classroom of hard knocks, or you could simply call it life.

Instead of a life with a bumper sticker on my back reading— "stronger every day," my life has looked more like this: Try and fail. Fail then try. Try and succeed. Succeed then fail. Two steps forward. One step back. One step forward. Three steps back. Every year, I get better at some things, worse at others. Some areas remain stubbornly static. To complicate matters even more, when I honestly acknowledge those ways in which I've gotten worse, it's actually a sign that I may be getting better. And when I become proud of the ways I've gotten better, it's clearly a sign that I've gotten worse. And 'round and 'round we go. Some people have always struggled with Saint Paul's admission that he did the things he knew he shouldn't, and he didn't do the things he knew he should. But I know exactly what he's talking about. The truth is, my life over the years doesn't look like a strong person getting stronger or a good person getting better—it looks like a weak and lost person who needs the strength and goodness of God.

Yeah, who can deliver me? Not me.

We love to believe that we are better than we are, stronger than we are, more capable, more spiritual, and more faithful than we are. We feel more valuable and important if we can convince ourselves of these things. We are all, in other words, high anthropologists by nature.

But this overinflated view of ourselves is actually enslaving. What happens when the giants we face always seem to win? What happens when we can't overcome the addiction for more than a week; when we can't seem to beat our anger problem; when no matter how hard we try, we can't seem to tame our tongue or get past our anxiety or stay faithful or escape our fears or make him/her love us?

What happens when no amount of positive thinking can scale the wall of guilt and shame you feel down deep? Have you ever tried to strong-arm yourself out of sadness? Have you ever tried to talk yourself out of your insecurities? Have you ever tried to will yourself out of loneliness or muscle your way out of feeling rejected? How did that go?

Real slavery is self-reliance—trying to be the currently-popular-but-eternally-problematic "hero of my own story." The only thing that can set us free from the bondage of relying on ourselves is coming face-to-face with our own deficiencies. Know thyself.

> Everyone is screwed up, broken, clingy, and scared, even the people who seem to have it more or less together. They are much more like you than you would believe. So try not to compare your insides to their outsides.
>
> —Anne Lamott

If all this sounds like a massively depressing start to a book, it isn't meant to be one. Quite the opposite. If I am grateful for anything about these past twenty years, it's for the way God has removed the idealistic scales from my eyes about myself and the world around me and replaced them with a realistic vision about the extent of his grace and love, which is much deeper and wider than I had ever imagined.

Indeed, the smaller you get—the smaller life makes you—the easier it is to see the grandeur of grace. That's not a statement about diminishing yourself, some variation of self-hatred (because that's the last thing we need). No, it's a confession in favor of what the Apostle Peter called being "sober-minded." In other words, having the self-awareness to admit that while I am far weaker and more screwed up than I may have initially thought, God has proven to be far stronger and more merciful than I could've ever dreamed. Knowing that *is* freedom.

I ONCE WAS FOUND BUT NOW I'M LOST

I think about the "lost" parables in Luke 15—lost sheep, lost coin, and lost son. The lost, or prodigal, son is the most familiar. I now refer to Luke's unforgettable parable as that of the prodigal **sons** (plural). We've taken that timeless story and unfortunately fixated on the obvious, the younger son who high-tailed it with his share of the inheritance to a far country and spent it all on wine, women, hard partying, and God knows what else. But the truth is the older brother was just as lost in his own far country, one within spitting distance of his father's back door, as he pouted because his younger brother returned to have his cake and eat it too. But both sons are lost. Both are dead in different but similar ways. Both are in the grip of a cruel and oppressive existence—the tyranny of their own far countries.

But get this—both sons started out in the house, right? Both were found, so to speak, but then got lost. And that same reality plays out in the two lesser-known parables in Luke 15.

In both of those cases, the lost sheep and the lost coin were at one time *not lost*. The lost sheep was in the fold, and the lost coin was in the pocket. The lost sheep wandered off, and the lost coin was misplaced. Again, the point I'm making is that neither started off lost. So, to interpret these parables as instructional guides on the lengths we "found-people" should go to find the "lost-people" (the way I was taught) is to misinterpret them. Not to mention, it downplays the reality of how quickly and easily we all get lost along the way. "Prone to wander, Lord, I feel it." Rather than these parables being about God's job description for us, they portray God's unflagging commitment to constantly come after those who once were found but now are lost.

To put it bluntly, these aren't parables about found people pursuing lost people. These are parables about God pursuing found people who get lost.

To deny that we all get lost is to blind our eyes to the truth about ourselves and others. We often, for example, get lost in our pursuit of meaning or love or success or purpose or importance. We get lost in our dependence on people and things to "save" us from aloneness, insecurity, and a sense of inadequacy. We get lost when hopes and dreams crash and burn—when one of our children goes off the deep end, when our parents get divorced, when a marriage fails, when she breaks up with you, when you don't get the job you want or get into the school you want. We get lost in anger, hurt, ambition, bitterness, pleasure-seeking, self-righteousness, unforgiveness, pride, lust, selfishness, the thirst for credit, the need to be right, and so on.

But the good news—I'd wager to say the great news—for me and for all of us in the dizzying light of these parables is that God spares no expense to find us *in* our lostness. He meets us in all our meanderings—seventy times seven. When we foolishly wander off, he comes after us, picks us up, puts us over his shoulders, and carries us home—every time! No matter how far you run, or how stubborn your roaming may be, he will never stop coming for you with infinite amounts of grace at the ready and forgiveness on the house. His pursuant love is mugging in nature. And he doesn't chide us for getting lost—he seeks us, finds us, rejoices, and throws a party.

Robert Capon sums up these two parables poetically in *Kingdom, Grace, Judgment* when he writes:

> The entire cause of the recovery operation in both stories is the shepherd's, or the woman's, determination to find the lost. Neither the lost sheep nor the lost coin does a blessed thing except hang around in its lostness. On the strength of these parables, therefore, it is precisely our sins, and not our goodnesses, that most commend us to the grace of God. These parables of lostness . . . are emphatically not stories designed to convince us that if we will wind ourselves up to some acceptable level of moral and/ or spiritual improvement, God will then forgive us; rather they are parables about God's determination to move before we do—in short, to make lostness the only ticket we need to the Supper of the Lamb.[6]

Two sobering things I've learned since my own personal collapse are (1) you are capable of getting lost in a way that is unthinkable to you right now, and (2) God's love and forgiveness are big enough to cover the fact that your greatest failure may be ahead of you.

To downplay our proclivity to get lost is a kind of myopic naivete that is an enemy to grace. It's a tyranny. And by telling you more of my story in the pages to follow, I'm here to do my part to dismantle that tyranny. I'm here to be a witness to the reckless, raging fury that they call the love of God—thank you, Rich Mullins. Yes, I'm part of the resistance. That's the spirit of the book you hold in your hands.

And the response to tyranny of every sort . . .must always be this: dismantle it. Take it apart. Scatter its defenders and its proponents, like a flock of starlings fed to a hurricane.

—Barry Lopez, *Resistance*

GOD'S MISFITS AND THE MISFIT GOD

There's a pivotal scene in the movie *Bohemian Rhapsody* where a music industry executive is meeting the band Queen for the first time. This was still early in the Queen timeline; they'd not yet signed a record deal. The music executive looks at Freddie Mercury (Queen's lead singer) and says (and I'm paraphrasing), "So, tell me—what makes Queen any different from all the other bands I meet?" Mercury's answer was worth the price of admission:

> I'll tell you what it is, Mr. Reid. We're four misfits who don't belong together and we're playing for other misfits. They're the outcasts at the back of the room and we're pretty sure they don't belong either. We belong to them.[7]

I love that because that's exactly the way I feel! That's who I am—an outcast who belongs to the other outcasts at the back of the room. We're outcasts cast together by the God who seeks out the found and the lost and the guilty and the fearful and the hurting. We're card-carrying members of God's lunatic fringe. We're a bunch of misfits who belong to each other, and more importantly, we belong to the misfit God.

Misfit God? Yes.

In parable after parable, Jesus reveals a God who chooses to love all the wrong people: the defiant son, not the compliant one;

those who broke religious laws, not those who kept them; the hungover late-day workers, not the diligent all-day workers. We see "bad" people getting rewarded, "good" people getting rebuked, and everybody's idea of who the winners and losers are being turned upside down. Jesus was always making the merit mongers mad because he befriended, loved, and touched the outcast, the leper, the liar, the cheater, the sexually deviant.

He didn't do what he was supposed to do, go where he was supposed to go, or say what he was supposed to say. What made the religious fit-ins furious was Jesus' derelict habit of loving sinners. As Mike Yaconelli wrote, "According to his critics, Jesus 'did God' all wrong."[8]

Grace always, always provokes those who think they're good, those who think they're better, those with a high anthropology.

Jesus loving and embracing the falsely accused, the victim, and the one who is not guilty . . . that's *not* scandalous. In fact, that's expected. What *is* scandalous is that Jesus loved the criminal caught in the act, the assailant with blood on his hands, the one who reeks of guilt—filthy rich Zacchaeus, the woman caught in an adulterous embrace, even the Roman soldiers blithely tossing dice in the shadow of his dying body.

The good news of God's love and forgiveness is not just for those who are bullied and brokenhearted, but for perpetrators themselves. Not just for theoretical sinners, but for actual flesh-and-blood repeat offenders. You see, what offends us most about Jesus is not who he leaves out but rather who he lets in. The fact that his heart gravitates toward and embraces the immoral, the criminal, the blamable, the scoundrel, the pariahs and dregs of society—that is what makes him such a misfit God.

Grace itself is not expensive. It's not even cheap. It's free. A no-strings-attached gift of one-way love. But to *practice* grace—to love the unlovable, to forgive the unforgivable, to stand with the guilty—well, that might cost you favor and friends. It might just cost you your life. Grace, as Robert Capon writes in the preface to *Romance of the Word*, is:

> . . . wildly irreligious stuff. It's more than enough to get God kicked out of the God union that the theologians have formed to keep him on his divine toes so he won't let the riffraff off scot-free. Sensible people, of course, should need only about thirty seconds of careful thought to realize that getting off scot-free is the only way any of us is going to get off at all.[9]

A misfit God indeed.

GRACE, ALWAYS GRACE

There is a huge life-and-death difference between religion and grace. Religion focuses primarily on us and how we live. Religion, in this sense, is not about God at all. It's about me and what I should do (or shouldn't do). It's about my performance, my obedience, my faithfulness, my potential, my strength, my improvement, and so on. Religion's main message is our need to do more, try harder, get better, and climb higher for God. It makes faith all about earning and deserving and getting paid handsomely for a job well-done. It has no room for failure and weakness. It may give lip service to God hanging on a cross for us, but its emphasis is you and me climbing a ladder for him. I've found it to be terribly narcissistic, an exercise in spiritualized navel-gazing—slavery, really.

The liberating antithesis of the performance-driven focus of religion is grace.

Grace asserts that true faith is not about our half-assed movement toward God, it's about God's wholehearted movement toward us. It embraces the beautiful truth that because of what God has done for us, there is nothing we can do—or fail to do—that will ever tempt him to leave us, forsake us, or stop loving us. God's love for us, acceptance of us, and commitment to us does not ride on our devotion to him but rather on his devotion to us. God's relationship to us is not grounded on what's in our hearts for him, but rather what's in his heart for us. In other words, what keeps us connected to God is not that we hold tightly to him, but that he holds tightly to us even when, and possibly especially when, we let go. We are safe and sound in his love because of his faithfulness, not ours. That is great news because religion's emphasis on doing good, being good, and getting better is exposed for the unhelpfulness that it is when everything falls apart.

It's never easy to admit our failures and flaws, to confess our sins and struggles. It's hard to share our secrets and talk about our insecurities. In a world that values strength, it's difficult to acknowledge weakness. Telling the truth about ourselves is scary. So, we edit our profiles. We wear masks. We conceal our most unattractive parts. We lie to ourselves, and we lie about ourselves, all because we are terrified that if people really knew us, they wouldn't love us.

Therein lies the beauty of grace. It sets you free to talk truthfully about yourself without fear because the only person's approval you ultimately need is God's, and you already have it. You can endure rejection from others because you'll never have to endure rejection from God. Those who are the most free are those who have the least fear telling the truth about themselves. And those who have the least fear telling the truth about themselves are those who know how much God loves them unconditionally.

The good news of God's grace rings true when we are finally able to admit that we are weak and we need help, that we fail, that we're not as put-together as we want people to think we are. That's when the rushing wind of mercy blows through and reminds us of how beloved we are no matter what. No. Matter. What.

The god of religion would have given up on us a long time ago: *one and done*. But the God of grace is the deity category killer: *his love never ceases*. He indiscriminately accepts us, the recidivist screwups, again and again and again. He's the shepherd constantly searching. The woman desperately looking high and low. The hope-filled father running with outstretched arms crying, "Welcome home." Again, and again, and again.

Grace, always grace.

Chapter 2
NOT MY FIRST RODEO

I suppose we're all drunk on something.

—Seth Haines, *Coming Clean*

If you've made a mess of your life (like I have), then you probably struggle with a lot of guilt, shame, and regret (like I do). And if you're a parent and the mess you've made has hurt your kids, then the guilt, shame, and regret you probably feel is often paralyzing (like mine is).

Mess isn't the right word. I mean it is, but it isn't. A mess is spilling an entire pitcher of orange juice at breakfast in your mother-in-law's lap. Or entering the wrong destination airport code when you're buying tickets for that romantic getaway weekend. Messes—they're a pain in the ass, an embarrassment; they can be a legitimate major headache, but they can be cleaned up, fixed, rescheduled. A quick thesaurus search of synonyms for "making a mess" reveals: *blundered, botched, goofed, mishandled, ruined, screwed up.* Now let your mind go to the "pointing Rick Dalton" meme from *Once Upon a Time in Hollywood*, the one where DiCaprio sits up, beer and cigarette in hand, and points to the television with a shock of recognition. That's what I felt when I came across "screwed up." There, that's it! That's what I did. I didn't make a mess. Oh no, I screwed up.

There hasn't been a day since I became a dad nearly thirty years ago that I have not wanted to be a dad. There have been times when I didn't want to be a husband, a friend, a son, or a brother. But I have always loved being a father to my three kids: Gabe, Nate, and Genna. From the moment each of them came into this world, we've been close. Parenting has had its share of challenges and heartaches over the years, but being a dad has not been hard for me. It's been my life's deepest joy since I became one.

So, when I had to sit down in 2015 and tell my three children that I had been unfaithful to their mother, Kim, it was the worst moment of my life. I will never, ever forget the details of that occasion. They are etched in my memory as if it happened twenty minutes ago. The looks on their faces, their words, their tears. To this day, every particular part of that Friday afternoon haunts me. It wasn't so much that time stood still as time slowed down to the slightest pulse possible without stopping.

My daughter Genna was the first to speak. With a look of utter sadness, shock, and disappointment, she said, "Dad, why? Why? Why did you do this? I trusted you. You're my dad. We are supposed to be best friends."

Nate didn't say a word. He looked down with his lip quivering, and then got up and walked out the front door.

Then Gabe, my oldest, spoke. Holding his brand-new baby boy (my grandson Mason) with his wife sitting next to him, he shot me a look of anger and deep sadness and said, "I've always looked up to you. You are my dad. You are my mentor. I tell everybody that you are my mentor. Dad, I can't believe you did this."

At that time, all three of my kids were already in a very fragile place. Genna was heading into her final year of middle school, Nate had just graduated from high school and was headed off to college, and Gabe had just started his little family. Never had they needed their dad more, and there I was delivering further hurt into their already delicate lives.

They had grown up in a tight-knit, fun-loving home. From the moment they came into this world, Kim and I loved them as best as we could. We persistently pointed them to God, but humanly speaking we were their foundation, their security. I had done my best to protect them, comfort them, provide for them, bear their burdens, teach them, and make them laugh. The fact that I had failed them, crushed them, and forever altered their lives is a guilt-ridden ache I will never outlive. Never. I screwed everything up. My own damn fault.

NOT THE FIRST TIME

What my children and Kim didn't know at the time was that my admission of the affair that outed me wasn't the first time I'd cheated on Kim. I'd been unfaithful before 2015. I used to think that unfaithfulness in marriage—*infidelity*—was a category reserved for those who had been physically or sexually unfaithful to their spouse. Not anymore. As I said in the Prologue, my understanding of what it means to be adulterous is much wider than it used to be and includes things like thoughts, feelings, and non-sexual behavior.

Years earlier, I had reconnected with an old girlfriend from high school. We were in touch for a particular reason that had nothing

to do with rekindling an old flame. She asked for my help and
advice on a project she was working on. It was all business. Even
though she had been my "first love," there was nothing about our
communication initially that even seemed wrong or dangerous. We
lived in different parts of the country. We were both married with
kids and committed to our families. We said nothing inappropriate
to each other. From every angle, it appeared harmless, innocent
even. After all, it had been over twenty years since we were close.
But as the conversations continued, feelings eventually started to
flow that made me realize something was missing in my marriage,
a kind of conversation and emotional connection that I wanted in
a marriage that didn't seem to be happening in mine at the time.
Looking back, I think my marriage had stronger connections than I
realized, and I take full responsibility for not seeing them. Perhaps
I chose not to see them. After all, I could have asked for a closer
connection, worked for it too, but suddenly here it was, ready-made
in an old girlfriend, and we could simply pick up where we left off.
Delusional? Absolutely. Did it feel real? Yes, it did.

　　After a couple months of conversation, we realized this had to
stop. If things had continued, it wasn't going to end well for either
of us. Although my heart was swirling, I did have the presence
of mind to know this was dangerous. We both did. And so, our
communication ended. We were never physical in any way, so
technically I didn't cheat. But those technicalities don't hold water
with your wife, your kids, your friends, not to mention God. I had
crossed an emotional line. I had opened a door. My reconnection
with this old girlfriend had tapped into a longing, creating a
romantic hunger that would not go away even after all contact
had ended. In fact, I don't think I really wanted it to go away. The
longing itself made me feel emotionally alive. But I was adulterous

in my heart. It's not that the longing is wrong, for that's intensely human and, I believe, woven into each one of us. It's what you do with the longing, how you handle it, where you take it. Or where you let it take you.

I brought the longing back home, so to speak, and for a while all of that stirred-up romantic energy was channeled to Kim, my wife. In fact, the next eight months or so were some of the best months of marriage I had ever experienced. I even thought quietly to myself that reconnecting with my old girlfriend had reconnected me to my marriage—strange and silly and delusional as that sounds, a variation of what the writer Joan Didion called "magical thinking." But as time went on, Kim and I resumed our normal rhythms, the way we'd grown accustomed to living with one another. She, of course, knew nothing about what I had done. Nobody did. But the past was now the past, and I felt like I had dodged a bullet. It actually felt like God had rescued me from blowing it big by allowing me to blow it small. I had experienced a divine warning shot, a warning that worked at first, but the magic wore off in time.

Not long afterward, I found myself in a peak season professionally. I was getting attention from a lot of people in a lot of places, both inside and outside religious circles. People wanted to hear what I had to say. My popularity was skyrocketing. Things were grooving; it felt like a winning season. Fame began to snowball. It was 2014, in the spring, that time of the year traditionally when kings go off to war.

> In the spring of the year, the time when kings go out to battle, David sent Joab, and his servants with him, and all Israel. And they ravaged the Ammonites and besieged Rabbah. But David remained at Jerusalem.
>
> —2 Samuel 11:1 ESV

That little detail—"But David remained at Jerusalem"—is crucial. In a nutshell, David wasn't where he was supposed to be. And neither was I. Now from the outside looking in, it appeared I was right where I should be. As I said, it was a winning season. The metrics we most commonly use to evaluate ourselves, especially those in leadership roles of any kind? I was checking the boxes. But don't forget, I had an adulterous heart. And beginning in the spring of 2014, my prone-to-wander heart was in full swing.

HEDONIC TREADMILL

Experts in the field of positive psychology and happiness use a phrase to describe the very human tendency to keep chasing something more pleasurable or better in life, and once we attain it, we become insensitive, or adapt, to the new and then need something more intense than the last in order to scratch that itch. Whatever progress we thought we might have made, we realize (if we have the presence of mind) that we're back in the same place. We've gone nowhere really, thus their phrase "the hedonic treadmill."

As far back as I can remember, I've been on the treadmill. I can't say I knew it, simply that I was running. I always wanted more than what I had. Even though I had been given so much, it never felt like enough. I was always looking past wherever I was or whoever I was with for something better.

As a teenager, regardless of where I was, who I was with, or what I was doing, something better and more exciting had to be around the bend, right? I was always looking for more fun, more adventure, more freedom, something more exciting. Now some of that I attribute to being a teenager, being young. The hunt for more is a facet of youth. But left unexamined and unchecked, unchallenged even, that hunger for more follows you into adulthood, where the stakes are infinitely higher.

As I got older, it became increasingly hard to enjoy the season of life I was in because I kept looking ahead to the next one. As a college student, I couldn't wait to get to graduate school. When I was in graduate school, I couldn't wait to get on with my career. Not long after I took my first job out of seminary, I was thinking ahead to what my next job would be. As a pastor, Sundays were the carrot dangling on the stick—I always wanted next Sunday to be bigger than last Sunday, the next sermon to be better than the last sermon. As an author, I always wanted the next book to be better and to sell more than the last book. Hedonic treadmill, indeed.

But here's the deal. As the church grew and I became well-known for my preaching skills and my books became bestsellers, it still wasn't enough. It didn't seem to matter that I was on TV and radio, getting invitations to speak at the biggest churches and conferences, and receiving widespread recognition and respect for my work—something more, something better (I believed), had to be around the corner. I was always reaching for something just beyond my grasp, always looking for a higher landscape, always striving for the next level. Some spiritual circles speak of "holy discontent" that reflects a restlessness that supposedly spurs you on to do more with your life for God and others. Yeah, this ain't that. This was *unholy* discontentedness. In *The Moviegoer*, Walker Percy captures the essence of my discontent:

> What is the nature of the search? you ask. Really
> it is very simple, at least for a fellow like me; so simple
> that it is easily overlooked. The search is what anyone

would undertake if he were not sunk in the everydayness of his own life. This morning, for example, I felt as if I had come to myself on a strange island. And what does such a cast away do? Why he pokes around the neighborhood and he doesn't miss a trick. To become aware of the search is to be onto something. Not to be onto something is to be in despair.[10]

There are definitely nuances, but there is a difference between being "onto something" as Percy says which rouses you to "the search," and being "on something" like a treadmill which leaves you ultimately sunk.

Throughout human history, philosophers and sages couldn't help noticing this longing, the proverbial hole in our hearts, the universal and insatiable yearning to experience *more*, something higher, deeper, fuller, richer, stronger, more enlivening. We're cravers— we crave full acceptance and favor, we crave lasting affection and approval, we crave meaning and purpose. And we spare no expense to find what we're looking for. Everybody's got a hungry heart.

Aristotle put it pithily when he said, "It is the nature of desire not to be satisfied, and most human beings live only for the gratification of it."[11]

Observing this phenomenon about himself, Saint Augustine caught this perhaps most famously and succinctly sixteen centuries ago on the opening page of his *Confessions*, where he prayed, "You made us for yourself, O God, and our hearts are restless until they rest in you."[12]

Twelve centuries after Augustine, the brilliant mind of Blaise Pascal took up this same human predicament. "All men seek happiness," he noted in his *Pensées;* "this is the motive of every action of every man, even of those who hang themselves." He then went on to cite humanity's endless sighs and groans as confirmation that nobody ever really satisfies this innate desire: "All complain—princes and subjects, noblemen and commoners, old and young, strong and weak, learned and ignorant, healthy and sick, of all countries, all times, all ages, and all conditions."[13]

Such universal dissatisfaction ought to convince us "of our inability to reach the good by our own efforts," Pascal says, but it's a lesson we fail to grasp: "And thus, while the present never satisfies us, experience dupes us," and so onward we stumble "from misfortune to misfortune . . . seeking from things absent the help [we do] not obtain in things present. But these are all inadequate . . . because the infinite abyss can only be filled by an infinite and immutable object, that is to say, only by God Himself."[14]

What Pascal describes as "seeking from things absent the help he does not obtain in things present" resonates with me. That's been me my whole life. Maybe you too. Maybe all of us.

Aristotle. Augustine. Pascal. Percy. All these brilliant minds saw this restlessness within the human condition. But this reality is old, older than Aristotle and Augustine. I mean, this goes back all the way to our origin stories, to the God who dreamed all this, including us, into being. As a Christian, I hold to the story about a garden, one that held everything we could ever want or need. But the temptation for something more was too great to resist, and whether it was an apple or a peach or an ear of sweet corn, the fruit in question was good and pleasing to the eyes, and desirable for gaining autonomy: "You will be like God." So, we disregarded the warnings, reached out, and took a bite. And that changed everything going forward, for all of us.

Ultimately, in my case, the thirst for what I thought I didn't have caused me to lose everything I did have. And again, to a large degree, I was unaware of what was truly going on. I was not "onto something" but "on something"—on the treadmill, at high speed, blindfolded. Yes, a recipe for disaster.

In my season of adultery, I selfishly wanted to be known and loved and affirmed in a way that I felt I wasn't experiencing in my own marriage at the time. It's not that those dynamics were wholly absent, but still, I wanted more. And rather than reveling in and resting on the fact that I was already *fully* known, *fully* loved, and *fully* affirmed by God—thereby setting me free from needing anything more from anyone else—I went lookin' for more in all the wrong places.

> Like a river that don't know where it's flowing,
> I took a wrong turn and just kept going.
>
> —Bruce Springsteen

I engaged in a handful of conversations and developed a few relationships with other women during that time, but most of those conversations and relationships would have been considered innocent because there was nothing sexual about them, because that's not what I was looking for. But they were far from guiltless. No matter how hard I tried to convince myself that talking and responding to these women was okay because, after all, I wasn't sleeping around, I knew it was questionable at best, dangerous at worst. Feeling new and exciting to someone is, well, exciting. The attention, the admiration—it all felt so affirming, so enlivening. Being freshly discovered and noticed can be distractingly (and destroyingly) intoxicating. So, like a drunken fool, I kept drinking.

In my winning season, I received all sorts of communication from people. I felt like the rhinestone cowboy—"getting cards and letters from people I don't even know." Many of these arrived via email, and my assistant at the time helped me with responses. At that time, I had two email accounts—one general and one more private, but both on the church's server, nothing secretive, just different accounts. Emails to my general account went straight to my assistant. Emails to my private account came only to me.

One day, my assistant received an email on my general account that she forwarded to my private account, a complimentary note from a very articulate woman. I responded from my private account with a standard "thank you so much." Then, she emailed again, telling me how she'd read one of my books and was experiencing some freedom she'd never had before having grown up in a strict religious environment. I responded with a "thank you" once more. And then, she emailed again, this time telling me she and her husband were members of a church about thirty minutes north of where I was a pastor, but she wasn't satisfied with the preaching there. She went on to tell me that one Sunday, unbeknownst to me, they visited Coral Ridge. She said she loved it and found my message to be smart and freeing; then she made a comment about how attractive she thought I was. Well, that was it. Those specific affirmations scratched me right where I itched.

Before I responded, I looked her up and found that in addition to being incredibly articulate, she was incredibly beautiful. If her compliments of me were her way of fishing, then I was ready, willing, and happy to be caught. A day or two later, I emailed her back and gave her my phone number. She texted me right away, and that started a conversation far from whatever guardrails email might provide. We were, at that point, off to the races.

Over the next few weeks, we met a total of four times, always in public places and always during the day, except for the first time. We talked and talked a lot. We talked about life, God, family, music, books. We both grew up in the church and had almost identical frustrations with it. Our conversations were stimulating. And while we never slept together, we were physical.

I'll never forget driving home after our first kiss. I was simultaneously scared to death and stirred with excitement. I knew I had done something that could cost me everything—that I had crossed another line—but it also made me feel more alive.

The first time we met was in a parking lot at the beach. She parked a hundred yards or so from where I was parked and came to sit in my car. We sat there for about forty-five minutes and during that time, she got a parking ticket. A few weeks later, her husband found the payment for the ticket, which revealed she wasn't where she'd told him she was that night, and she confessed she'd met me to talk. In quick succession, I got a phone call from her husband: "Tullian, we need to meet."

Yes, this is the point in the made-for-TV movie where the betrayed husband loses his shit and goes berserk on the other guy, and somebody ends up with their skull crushed in, usually the other guy. Well, we met at a Starbucks and thankfully he didn't kill me. But he did say plainly: "Don't do it again." At that point, he only knew about the one meeting. What he didn't know was that she and I had also met three times after she got the parking ticket. He also didn't know the physical details of our relationship, and the frequency of our communication over the previous weeks. I was hoping he'd never find out about that stuff. I assured him that I would never meet with her again, and I didn't. We never met after that. As far as I was concerned, I had dodged another bullet, although this one had grazed me.

Fast-forward a few weeks. I was on a trip and got a call from a very good friend of mine—an older, wise mentor who has known me my whole life. He told me that he had received a message from a pastor in Kentucky, a former student of his who happened to be this woman's father (no, I'm not making this stuff up). The son-in-law had told his wife's father what happened between his daughter and me. And since the father knew who I was and knew that his former professor was a close friend of mine, he reached out and told him. So, my friend (still with me?) called me to find out what was going on and to gauge whether there was any truth to what this man had said. I downplayed the whole thing significantly, telling my friend it was just a one-time meeting, that nothing happened, and that if I was guilty of anything, it was simply a momentary lapse of reason (spoken like a blind man on a treadmill). My friend bought it. He then told me that this father was not happy, and that he wanted me to call him. I assured my friend that I would.

Yes, this is that point in the movie when if the betrayed husband rained mercy on you, the angry father brings justice's thunder.

Fearful of what I was going to find on the other side of the phone, I called the father and found him to be surprisingly gracious. He was, of course, upset and made it very clear to me how foolish I had been. But he was rational and kind. He too only knew about the one meeting and, like her husband, knew nothing about the physical nature of our relationship and the constancy of our communication during that time. I feigned sorrow and contrition, and he bought what I was selling. Although I was in full damage control mode, here I'd dodged yet another bullet.

A MIDSUMMER NIGHT'S NIGHTMARE

Skip ahead a month or so to midsummer 2014. I'd had no communication of any kind with this woman, and in my mind I had successfully appeased both the husband and the father (emphasis on *in my mind*). I figured this was now firmly behind me. Then I received a text out of the blue from her now-fuming father: "I know everything. I just read through every text message you exchanged with my daughter, and the two of you significantly minimized what actually happened." My heart sank; it was jarring, like the treadmill skipped a gear or something. Those texts were a smoking gun—indisputable, damning evidence of a much more involved relationship than what anybody knew up until then. I could tell this wasn't going away.

I was on vacation with my family, and needless to say, mine was over. I subsequently received a message from our mutual friend who'd been contacted by the now-fuming father who wanted the three of us to meet in person in Orlando. I'm not sure I've ever been as scared as I was in that moment.

We met, the three of us, and her father raked me over the coals (as he should have). The "treadmill" was now shaking violently, like a boat on stormy waves. I was losing my footing, and then he essentially pulled the power cord from the wall so that everything came to a screeching halt—he read me a letter his son-in-law had written to me. It was well written and maturely tempered, but at the same time scathing and surgical. It's been many years since that letter was read to me, but I do remember one line of it in particular. He sweetly described how much he loved his wife's soft, full lips and how they were designed specifically for his enjoyment but that I had now stolen that from him. By the time the father finished reading the letter, I was down, completely and totally. A little while earlier I was more afraid than I'd ever been, but in that moment, I was more ashamed than I can ever remember. I was no longer feigning contrition and sorrow. Now I felt it. Truly. I looked at my life and wondered *How could I have done this? Who even am I? What have I become?*

I was expressly undone, and this angry preacher-father who would have been justified in showing me the back of his hand offered me a grace and forgiveness that drove me to my knees. He accepted my apology and confession, and then asked me to leave the room so he could talk to my friend alone. After a few minutes, the father came out of the room, put his hands tenderly on my shoulders, prayed for me, and said, "This is finished. We have followed the process laid out in Matthew 18, and there is therefore no need to take this any further. It's behind us now."

Wouldn't that make for a cinematic conclusion, something darkly Hallmarkian? But that wasn't the end. I thought it was. He thought it was. My mentor friend thought it was. But it wasn't.

About a month and a half later, I was at a lunch meeting and got a text from my friend saying, "Call me ASAP," and that jarring, heart-sinking feeling hit me again. I called, and he told me that the pastor of the nearby church this woman and her husband attended, who had been counseling them, felt I needed to tell at least a couple of the elders of my church what had happened, and if I didn't, they were going to. This felt like some perverse Groundhog Day skit.

With fear and trepidation, I promptly arranged a meeting in Fort Lauderdale between the now not-so-angry father-preacher, our mutual friend, and two elders from my church. All cards were on the table; no truth was withheld, and I apologized, again. The elders from my church were older, well-respected men who'd been there for decades and knew me well. After hearing the thorough testimony of the father and my confession, they asked to meet with me once a week going forward, which we did. As far as the husband of the woman, her father, and the pastor of their church were concerned, this matter was now closed. I started moving forward, tentatively. I was still scared because several people now knew what had happened.

There was one crucial person, however, who did not know about any of this: my wife, Kim.

For the next seven months or so I dealt with a lot of guilt, a good deal of shame, and a shitload of fear. I was terrified that this would somehow get out, and there were constant reminders that this was possible, even probable.

For example, during that time I got a call from one of the two elders at Coral Ridge who were a part of this. He told me that he had received a call from the pastor of the church where this woman and her husband attended. The pastor told him that a board member of his church who knew about the situation also served on the board of a large Christian university where I was scheduled to speak. This board member voiced concern to his pastor about me speaking and thought I should back out. He didn't threaten to blow the whistle if I didn't, but I was scared that he might. So, I made up some excuse as to why I had to cancel, and I canceled.

Fear wasn't steps away, crouching at the door. It had me in its jaws, swallowing me whole.

Chapter 3
LIFE IN THE FAST LANE

Like a dog that returns to its vomit is a fool who reverts to his folly.

—Proverbs 26:11 NRSV

There's a chance you might wonder if it's possible to be self-fooled into an even deeper foolery. The answer is yes. Like a vomit-loving-dog-fool, I reverted to my folly, this time in bold. In the previous affairs I mentioned, I crossed some lines. In my final, widely known and publicized affair, I crossed them all. Whatever "rules" yet remained to be broken, I broke them. *Faster, faster, the lights are turnin' red.*

I've mentioned a confession in June 2015, the one that shattered my kids, Kim (and others, including me). It was necessary because the night before, five elders from Coral Ridge showed up at my house. It was not a pastoral appreciation visit—far from it.

Two months earlier, in April 2015, I had requested from the elders a three-month leave of absence to address a marital crisis that needed my full attention, a crisis that, ironically, had nothing to do with my then undisclosed infidelities. They immediately granted it to me. But far from the crisis getting better, it got worse. And as a result of this worsening crisis, Kim and I separated.

It was pretty obvious to those in the know that my marriage was headed toward divorce. So about six weeks into my three-month leave of absence, the elder board approached me and made me an offer in exchange for my resignation—a plan to get me out quietly and quickly and hopefully avoid some negative press that eventually happened anyway. I was crushed and angry. My family and I needed our church family now more than ever, and it felt like they were abandoning us. I had been feeling the writing on the wall, but now I could see it. I felt I was being phased out, as a husband and also as a minister—two vital identity pieces for me. While I could have paused and responded in humble confession for any and all wrongs, I reacted instead like the angry toddler whose toys are taken away. I threw a fit.

It was during that leave of absence from Coral Ridge and subsequent separation from my wife that my affair in 2015 began—the one that ultimately outed me.

A woman entered my life during those separations—someone interested in me, someone I was interested in, someone who seemed to be on my side, so to speak. Of the affairs I had, she was the only one who had been a part of our church, even though neither of us was attending at the time our romance began. I read one blog post a while back that said I had been "involved in sexual misconduct with several congregants." That's just flat out false. Not a shred of truth to that. But the fact that I had entered into a relationship with someone who had been closely connected to our church does speak scarily of the progressive nature of my foolishness. I was now acting on my adulterous heart in my own backyard, as it were, a boundary that none of my previous affairs had transgressed.

Our relationship started as friends. But as my marriage (and hers) got rocky, we became close, then closer. Our romance began and continued consensually. There's one narrative out there that says our relationship started while I was counseling them in their marriage. That's absolutely not true. I never once counseled her and her husband. There's yet another narrative out there that says I groomed her, that I used my power differential to seduce her. I don't even know how to sensibly respond to that. She's a well-educated, bright, independent woman. To say she was somehow jedi-mind-tricked by me into having an affair is not only ludicrous and false, but an insult to her intelligence. We were two fully consenting adults who pursued one another, who freely chose one another. I fell for her. She fell for me. We, both of us, had been unfaithful to our spouses before—more than once. We, both of us, knew exactly what we were doing. Neither of us was a victim; our kids and spouses were. We were drawn to each other at first emotionally, then physically, and finally and fully sexually. For about six weeks, we saw one another almost every day, and if someone saw us together, I could have cared less. Remember, I was throwing a fit. My children and my mother (we were all living together while I was separated from my wife) could see that this was trouble. They did not like this woman coming around as often as she did, and they let me know as much. I had friends who registered the same concern: "Tullian, dude, this is not smart." But I didn't care. Or more accurately, I was so deep in my own rage, hurt, and selfishness that I couldn't be bothered to care. I actually thought at the time, delusional as I was, that this woman was a gift from God, a source of comfort to me while my own marriage seemed destined for divorce. Again, magical thinking.

I countered the severance offer from Coral Ridge, made some demands that set in motion a need on their part to have some kind of leverage. That advantage presented itself when text messages between this woman and me were discovered on the church's server. There was nothing sexually suggestive in the messages, but it was proof *something* was going on, a relationship with more than a whiff of impropriety. It was all they needed, and I knew it. We were busted. Game over.

When the elders from Coral Ridge showed up to my house at around 9:30 p.m. on Thursday, June 18, they had what they needed in hand—printouts of all my text messages with this woman. They were there to confront me and demand my resignation. Were there some he-said-she-said-they-said aspects to how the elders found out? You bet; that's how these things go, always. But beyond what someone may have said is what someone actually did, that someone being me. I, the young pedigreed pastor of one of America's most famous churches in an area of the country where image is like oxygen, got caught having an affair with a married woman, and it wasn't so much that I thought nobody would find out as I didn't care if they did. Sin unravels the lives of those who care for you; it always does. But most of all it unravels you, until you find yourself unrecognizable.

Not long after our relationship was exposed, I broke it off with this woman. It should've never started, and I knew it would only be worse for both of us if it continued. Six weeks after it began, it ended.

So, on Thursday, June 18, 2015, the elders of Coral Ridge Presbyterian Church showed up at my door. On Friday, June 19, 2015, I told my kids of this affair (the only one that was widely known at the time). On Sunday, June 21, 2015, that news became public. That cat was out of the bag, which is a sanitized way to say the shit hit the fan. I wonder sometimes if deep down that's what I wanted to happen all along . . . to finally get caught . . . so maybe the treadmill would finally just stop . . . *just dyin' to get off.*

You'd think a forty-two-year-old pastor would know better, act better, be better. But no. There was obviously a progression to my sin. It started with a woman far away, which didn't involve anything physical and ended with a woman close to home, which was sexual. But I pause at that word *progressive* because the reality is it was *regressive.* I'd regressed into something less, someone less. That's what sin does, it brings about a wasting.

Now, this may be more than you'd ever want to know about the ways particular churches operate, but it's like a load-bearing wall in my story—you can't take it out; it's there; it has to stay. In Presbyterian denominations, the governing body that maintains jurisdiction and authority over all the ministers in a particular region is called a "presbytery." So, while Coral Ridge (the church) could request my resignation, they didn't have the power to remove me as pastor; *only* the presbytery (governing body) could do that. I did eventually resign from Coral Ridge, but because I was still an ordained member of the presbytery, my case had to be dealt with. Stay with me here. So, the committee that handled disciplinary matters pertaining to ministers reached out to me and explained there were two steps to their plan: (1) I would write out a confession, and (2) I would have several phone calls and then a face-to-face meeting with the chairman of that committee. After I completed these steps, the committee would consider what was best going forward, landing on two possible disciplinary scenarios: (1) They could suspend me and begin a process of discipline and evaluation with the hope that at some point, I could be restored and reinstated as a pastor somewhere, albeit not at Coral Ridge, or (2) They could go the more expedient route and simply strip me of my pastoral credentials—"defrock" me, and I would no longer be a minister in the Presbyterian denomination in which I was ordained.

The presbytery met and decided on the second option. In light of my confession, they considered me unfit for ministry and stripped me of my credentials. They defrocked me. And in doing so, washed their hands of me and relinquished all jurisdiction over me. Because my situation was so public, a lot of people both inside and outside the religious community were watching the presbytery very closely to see what they would do, how they would handle this sensitive, high-profile situation. As you can imagine, the presbytery felt that pressure, and so a quick defrocking rather than a long, drawn-out disciplinary process was, for them, the most expedient thing to do.

There's a narrative out there in the small pond of religious news that claims a process of discipline was presented to me by the presbytery and I ran from it—that I "fled from justice." That made for a juicy story, but it never happened. At no point was I offered a formal process of discipline. My defrocking *was* the discipline. In fact, if they had presented me with some such process, chances are good I would have jumped through any prescribed hoops in order to get some semblance of my old life back. And I would have done so for all the wrong reasons. Little did I know that God had his own discipline and restoration process in store for me that would ultimately prove to be longer, wiser, more painful, more unpredictable, and infinitely more effective than anything any church or denomination could've come up with. God's like that, I've learned.

LOW ANTHROPOLOGY

It's probably wise to pause here a minute and answer a question that's no doubt blinking like a "check engine" light. And far from some kind of sidebar, this is core: *How can a person keep relapsing into the same destructive pattern of behavior? Or, to ask the same question using religious language: How can a Christian keep on sinning in the same way?*

Brennan Manning responded to this question in his classic *The Ragamuffin Gospel*. Manning was an ex-priest, sought-after speaker, acclaimed author, plus a card-carrying alcoholic. One of his more memorable benders happened after landing at Newark airport en route to his mother's funeral. He stopped by a liquor store on the way to his hotel. Once he checked into his hotel, he started drinking, and kept drinking and drinking until he blacked out. Yes, he missed his own mother's funeral. How in the world could such a thing happen? Manning wrote:

> It is possible because I got battered and bruised by loneliness and failure; because I got discouraged, uncertain, guilt-ridden, and took my eyes off Jesus. Because the Christ-encounter did not transfigure me into an angel. Because justification by grace through faith means I have been set in a right relationship with God, not made the equivalent of a patient etherized on a table.[15]

In his 2011 memoir, *All Is Grace*, the aging Manning compressed his answer down to just three words, just as true: "These things happen."[16] My response would be slightly different than Manning's, yet similar in spirit.

In the world of recovery, stress and pressure are listed as top factors in relapse. And I'm sure that played a part for me. Looking back, I can now see that my life was stretched too thin. I was doing too much and moving too fast. But the simplest and truest explanation as to why I kept sinning in the same way doesn't have to do primarily with what was going on outside of me, but rather what's always going on inside of me.

I've already mentioned Paul Zahl's phrase—"low anthropology." Simply stated, having a low anthropology means having a view of human nature that admits we all need help, from one another and ultimately from God. It maintains that we're not the good, strong, independent people we like to think we are. It's an honest assessment of the human condition. It looks at humankind realistically, not idealistically. And what it sees is that none of us are angels. We are all imperfect people with a host of limitations and deficiencies, moral and otherwise. We are all, in fact, comprehensively dislocated. Martin Luther described the state of humanity with the Latin phrase, "*homo incurvatus in se*," which means, man is curved in on himself. In other words, we are by nature self-absorbed and self-focused. We are all a barrel of selfish thoughts and desires and wants.

The history of this world and of our lives proves that we humans have a huge capacity for screwing up, a natural tendency toward self-defeating behavior, what Sigmund Freud called "*Thanatos*"—a universal and innate "death drive." In one of Edgar Allan Poe's short stories, "The Imp of the Perverse," he explores our self-destructive impulses and argues that knowing something is dangerous and wrong can be "the one unconquerable force" that makes us want to do it. How screwed up is that? Echoes of the Apostle Paul's words that "*the law stirs up sin.*" We make a habit of running blindfolded on the treadmill juggling knives.

In his book *Unapologetic*, Francis Spufford simply calls it **HPtFtU**—The Human Propensity to Fuck Things Up:

> What we're talking about here is not just our tendency to lurch and stumble and screw up by accident, our passive role as agents of entropy. It's our active inclination to break stuff, "stuff" here including moods, promises, relationships we care about, and our own well-being and other people's, as well as material objects whose high gloss positivity seems to invite a big fat scratch.[17]

So, while repeated ruinous behavior is foolish, hurtful, and inexcusable, it shouldn't be shocking. It shouldn't surprise us when fallen people keep falling down, and broken people keep breaking things. We should expect sinners to sin. Hell, even Saint Paul lamented that the things he knew he shouldn't do, he kept on doing (see Romans 7).

None of this, by the way, is an *excuse* for doing destructive stuff. But it does *explain* why we foolishly keep on doing destructive stuff. Again and again and again.

My devastating actions were catastrophic for me and many others, and there's no justification for my actions. I was responsible to make better choices, and I willfully ignored that responsibility, and people I love very much were hurt. No one wanders into these kinds of dark, compartmentalized corners because they want to hurt those they love. For example, I wasn't thinking about how my repeated selfishness would deeply wound my kids. Who knows, maybe if I had, I would've saved myself and countless others a lot of heartache. Maybe. But I was thinking about me—what I wanted, not what others needed. I was popular and was lovin' every minute of it. I lost my way, plain and simple, under the glaring lights of my success. The "Christ-encounter" didn't make me an angel either, nor do I believe that was ever God's intent. As with Brennan Manning and with me, and possibly with you—these things happen.

In *The Prodigal: A Ragamuffin Story*, Greg Garrett wrote that Manning resonated so profoundly with the parable of the prodigal son because "he had plenty of wandering on his ledger."

Don't we all. Garrett went on:

> Like many of us, Brennan [Manning] knew what it felt like to stray, to slip into mires of our own making, to wish we could go home. Like many of us he knew what it felt like to think you are unworthy, that you have worn out your welcome, that there is no home left at home. But Jesus' story of the son who insulted his father by demanding his inheritance while his father was still living, who shamed his father by blowing through that inheritance with wine and women until nothing was left, is a story of the purest grace and of a love that will never write us off.[18]

Eugene Peterson summed it up best: "When we sin and mess up our lives, we find that God does not go off and leave us—he enters into our trouble and saves us."[19] So he does. Every time.

TENDER MERCIES

Back to my kids. Since that Friday many years ago, we've had a lot to work through—we've had the hard conversations and cried the hard tears. Thankfully, through it all we have remained undetachably close and deeply connected. I deserved to lose the love and affection of my kids forever, but their love for me has never blinked. Not even for a second. I have apologized to each of them a hundred times, and they have tenderly reminded me over and over and over again that they forgive me. I delivered pain into their lives, and they delivered pardon into mine. I wrote a book titled *One Way Love*, and the line below is mine. But my children are the ones who have lived it and given it. My children graced me.

> Grace is being loved when you are unlovable.
>
> —Tullian Tchividjian, *One Way Love*

They all know how much I love them. And I know how much they love me. And yet, despite how many times they remind me of their love and forgiveness, I still struggle with guilt and shame and regret for how I hurt them. Regardless of how many happy days we've had since then or how many happy days we'll continue to have together, **that** day will always haunt me. It will always be a thorn in my side reminding me of the pain I caused three precious lives that were entrusted into my care. I've accepted that. It's not going away.

To be sure, I understand academically that there is a difference between guilt, shame, and regret. But from an existential standpoint, those three emotions are almost impossible to distinguish. You feel what you feel, and no amount of fine distinctions can help you not feel it. Guilt, shame, and regret all feel pretty much the same in crisis—like someone's heavy boot is standing on your neck.

And I don't know about you, but it doesn't matter how many Bible verses someone points out or how many times well-meaning people tell me to "forgive myself" because God has forgiven me, I still can't shake my insufferable sense of I-screwed-upness. Maybe I should be able to. After all, not only have my kids forgiven me, but I do believe God has forever settled all my debts and forgiven me of all my sins. I do believe that "as far as the east is from the west, so far does he remove our transgressions from us" (Psalm 103:12 NIV). I also know that it's not God who brings up forgiven sins. I believe that absolution is absolute and that God doesn't keep score. I know all this in my head, but that doesn't mean I always believe it in my heart. To be honest, more often than not, I don't. "I believe; help my unbelief" (Mark 9:24 ESV). After you've screwed up, at some point down the road, yes, it's good to stop hugging the cactus. But most times, even when you do, you still feel the needles. Maybe you can relate.

Perhaps, you too have failed miserably and people that you dearly love have been deeply damaged. Maybe you committed adultery, like me. Maybe you're an addict (alcohol, porn, drugs, shopping, social media, etc.). Maybe your kids have gone off the deep end and you blame yourself for leaving their father years ago and breaking up your home. Maybe you've been an emotional or physical abuser. Maybe you've been a workaholic and you're just now realizing that you've lost years with your now adult children—years you'll never get back. Maybe it's just a lifetime of pushing people away because you're combative and critical and always have to be "right" and you look up one day and realize you're all alone.

Whatever it is for you, if you struggle with guilt and shame and regret for the pain you have caused people that you love, then you know an inescapable throbbing. You may be doing something fun or productive when out of nowhere, like a tidal wave of raw emotion, it hits you. And you are transported right back to the unavoidable reality that your selfishness has decimated someone else—someone you love, someone who loves you.

PHANTOM PLEASURES

A number of years ago, I was driving my daughter Genna, who was 16 at the time, to her mom's. We both love music, and we both play it loud. We always have fun in my car enjoying our favorite songs together. At one point during our two-hour drive, I looked over and saw that Genna was crying.

I immediately turned the music down and asked, "What's the matter, honey?"

She said, "I'm sad." I asked her why.

She said, "I like the way life used to be. Life is broken now. I miss our whole family being together."

I took her hand in mine. I reminded her of how sorry I am for my role in breaking up our family, and how much I love her. As she always does, she sweetly assured me of her forgiveness and her love for me as well.

After a few moments of silence, I shared with her this word picture of how life now feels in the aftermath of my screwup.

"Genna, it feels like our whole family was in the car together back in 2015, speeding down the highway, and I fell asleep at the wheel. In a flash, we were spinning out of control. We hit the ditch and rolled, over and over. When the car finally stopped, the tires were up in the air, the windows shattered. Thankfully, God spared our lives, but we weren't okay, not okay at all. All of us lost something that day. An arm. A hand. A leg. We were alive, but we all lost a limb. That awful day we became amputees. That is our new normal."

For me, the difficulty of losing a limb is hard, but it's nothing compared to watching those I love deal with the loss of their limbs. It's my fault they now have to struggle through life as amputees. It was my hands on the family's steering wheel. But the loss of a limb is the loss of a limb whether it's your fault or someone else's. Whether someone shoots your finger off or you shoot your own finger off, you still have to deal with the pain of living with one less finger.

The loss of a limb has forever changed how I experience life. Some people feel sorry for me. Others stare. And still others say, "That's what you deserve for driving that way." But the real challenge is not the whispering voices out there but the accusing voices within. Every day, in ways great and small, I'm reminded of life before the accident, the way things used to be. Life when everything was the old normal, pre-crash, pre-loss when I stood on my own two feet.

I know life can never be what it was, but I wrestle with the desire to rewind the clock, keep the car between the white lines, and avoid disaster. I still struggle with trying to recover some measure of what I used to have. There's not a day that goes by that isn't colored by yesterday. I can't tell you how often I feel like a man without a home—some wanderer trying to find a recognizable sight or sound, something that I used to know and love.

Amputees speak of phantom pains in the limbs they no longer have. I get that. With me, it's like I experience phantom pleasures. The joy of holding yesterday in a hand that is no more. The pleasure of standing strong in the past on legs I no longer have. Phantom pleasures remind me of what I lost and caused others to lose as well.

After I explained all this to Genna, she said, "That's exactly the way I feel, Dad."

I have no doubt that's the way you may feel too. It may be the death of someone you love, a painful divorce that's left your family in shambles, or a debilitating disease. It could be that your son is in prison, your daughter won't speak to you, or a close friend has stabbed you in the back. Perhaps your kids are grown, and you desperately miss those simpler, sweeter days when they were small and your house was full every day with the people you love most. You may live with guilt and shame and regret and sadness because of a terrible decision (or a string of terrible decisions), and it has cost you everything you once held dear. Life, as you knew and loved it, is gone. Or, maybe you're just getting older, and your body doesn't work the way it used to, or you don't think you look as young and beautiful as you once did.

Whatever it is for you, at some level, you too live life as an amputee. You've lost a piece of yourself. What you once took for granted is gone. Ripped away. Cut off. In some way and at some point, you have lost (or are losing) something or someone you love.

I can't say anything that will make you feel better. There are no instant, microwaveable solutions to these deep human griefs. There's no "hack." And I can't make your missing limb grow back any more than I can my own.

But there is something I've learned the hard way: when our faith (or lack thereof) feels like a fight *against* the realities of our faults and pains instead of a resource for *accepting* them, we are on the wrong track. To put it positively, the grace of God gives you the freedom and space to feel what you're feeling rather than to deny it—to face the reality of what you've done rather than flee from it. It gives you the permission to not "stuff it" but to admit it, to be honest with yourself about it, to be real, to assimilate it—to recognize it rather than to resist it. Why? Because grace tells us that God isn't keeping score; he's not counting our sins against us. And this means that our deep need to think well of ourselves and to "accept" ourselves is eclipsed by the truth that God already thinks well of us and accepts us no matter what we've done or who we've hurt.

Our hope is not that we will (in this life) get past our guilt, shame, and regret. Rather, it is that God promises to be with us when we struggle with our guilt, shame, and regret. So, when you find yourself plagued and paralyzed by the pain you've caused, grace is there to remind you over and over that there is what C. S. Lewis called, "a deeper magic" behind the curtain of your faults. Behind that accusing, internal voice that whispers, "Look at what you've done!" is the absolving, external voice that shouts, "Look at what I'VE done!" God is forever there to repeat over and over to our forgetful and unbelieving hearts that he meets our guilt and shame and regret with his grace. Over and over and over again. God loves us. Unconditionally.

BASTARDS ALL

We're all bastards but God loves us anyway.

—Will Campbell

That was the response Baptist preacher Will Campbell gave when his agnostic friend, P. D. East, demanded a succinct definition of the gospel. A part of Will Campbell's story is that he became active in the Civil Rights movement in the mid-1950s. In 1957 he was the only white person to be invited by Martin Luther King to the founding of the Southern Christian Leadership Conference. There were four ministers who escorted the "Little Rock Nine" to Central High School in Little Rock, Arkansas—Campbell was one of the four. And in 1963, he joined MLK's sit-ins and marches in Birmingham, Alabama. But in 1965, Campbell's friend and Episcopal seminarian, Jonathan Daniels, was murdered by a white deputy sheriff named Thomas Coleman. The Baptist preacher was enraged. His agnostic friend, East, returned to that folksy definition of the gospel (recounted in Campbell's book *Brother to a Dragonfly*):

> "Come on, Brother. Let's talk about your definition. Was Jonathan a bastard?"
>
> I said I was sure that everyone is a sinner in one way or another but that he was one of the sweetest and most gentle guys I had ever known.
>
> "But was he a bastard?" His tone was almost a scream. "Now that's your word. Not mine. You told me one time that everybody is a bastard. That's a pretty tough word. I know. Cause I am a bastard. A born bastard. A real bastard. My Mamma wasn't married to my Daddy. Now, by god, you tell me, right now, yes or no and not maybe, was Jonathan Daniels a bastard?"
>
> I knew that if I said no he would leave me alone and if I said yes he wouldn't. And I knew my definition would be blown if I said no.
>
> So I said, "Yes."
>
> "All right. Is Thomas Coleman a bastard?"
>
> That one was a lot easier. "Yes. Thomas Coleman is a bastard."
>
> "Okay. Let me get this straight now. I don't want to misquote you. Jonathan Daniels was a bastard. Thomas Coleman is a bastard. Right? Which one of these two bastards do you think God loves the most?" His voice now was almost a whisper as he leaned forward, staring me directly in the eyes.
>
> I made some feeble attempt to talk about God loving the sinner and not the sin, about judgment, justice, and

brotherhood of all humanity. But P. D. shook his hands in a manner of cancellation. He didn't want to hear about that.

"You're trying to complicate it. Now you're the one who always told me about how simple it was. Just answer the question." His direct examination would have done credit to Clarence Darrow.

He leaned his face closer to mine, patting first his own knee and then mine, holding the other hand aloft in oath-taking fashion.

"Which one of these two bastards does God love the most? Does he love that little dead bastard Jonathan the most? Or does He love that living bastard Thomas the most?"

Suddenly everything became clear. Everything. It was a revelation. The glow of the malt which we were well into by then seemed to illuminate and intensify it. I walked across the room and opened the blind, staring directly into the glare of the streetlight. And I began to whimper. But the crying was interspersed with laughter. It was a strange experience. I remember trying to sort out the sadness and the joy. Just what was I crying for and what was I laughing for. Then this too became clear.[20]

Bastards all. But God loves us anyway.

HOW TO SAVE A DROWNING BASTARD

Drowning victims, especially adults, can be dangerous. Think about that for a minute. Envision that panicking adult, reaching out and clutching or grabbing for something, anything they think might save them. And if that *something* is a human rescuer, the drowning person can grab them and pull them under in order to push themselves up. It's a scenario so common there's a name for it—AVIR, Aquatic-Victim-Instead-of-Rescuer Syndrome. That's why emergency responders agree that if you see someone drowning, the best response you can make is to find something buoyant and throw it to them from the shore or a boat, somewhere a safe distance from the drowning victim. It's a little counterintuitive, especially because that's not how it plays in the movies. But the real heroes know throwing a drowning person something to hang onto can save more than one life.

> Drowning people
> Sometimes die
> Fighting their rescuers.
>
> —Octavia Butler

In the Spring and Summer of 2015, I was drowning, as was my marriage. I was flailing and clutching for something, anything. We both were. Kim wasn't trying to save me, nor was I trying to save her. Sadly, that tells you about all you need to know as to the state of our marriage at that moment. There are narratives out there about my behavior at that time that are in no way, shape, or form true. But this one is. In my frantic-drowning frame of mind, I grabbed the person closest to me—Kim—and pushed her down. The day my resignation from Coral Ridge due to moral failure was made public, *The Washington Post* reached out to ask me if I'd be willing to make a statement. Because of everything that was going on, I was sad, embarrassed, ashamed, and also royally pissed off. So, I was more than happy to oblige. We can say and do some damnably regrettable stuff when we're enraged, and I certainly did. I believe that's why the Apostle Paul cautioned: "In your anger, do not sin" (Ephesians 4:26 NIV). Here's my statement from the June 21, 2015, edition of *The Washington Post*:

> I resigned from my position at Coral Ridge Presbyterian Church today due to ongoing marital issues. As many of you know, I returned from a trip a few months back and discovered that my wife was having an affair. Heartbroken and devastated, I informed our church leadership and requested a sabbatical to focus exclusively on my marriage and family. As her affair continued, we separated. Sadly and embarrassingly, I subsequently sought comfort in a friend and developed an inappropriate relationship myself. Last week I was approached by our church leaders and they asked me about my own affair. I admitted to it and it was decided that the best course of action would be for me to resign. Both my wife and I are heartbroken over our actions and we ask you to pray for us and our family that God would give us the grace we need to weather this heart wrenching storm. We are amazingly grateful for the team of men and women who are committed to walking this difficult path with us. Please pray for the healing of deep wounds and we kindly ask that you respect our privacy.

Out of anger and rage, I outed my wife. If I was going down, she was going down with me. If the whole world was going to know about my screwup, then I was going to make sure they knew about hers too. Nice, huh? What a coward. Instead of protectively covering the mother of my children and owning **my** shit, I completely downplayed my adultery—"sought comfort in a friend" (dear God, give me a break)—and as has been rightly said, "threw her under the bus." I did, and I am extremely sorry for that. God knows how much I regret it. It was wrong, I was wrong. I wish there was a go-back-in-time machine so I could undo that bastard move. I wish there was, but there isn't. On top of all the other hurts I caused her, I hurt Kim even further with that, and I hate that I did. She knows how sorry I am and has graciously forgiven me. Since then, we've had hard talks and cried hard tears. We've apologized to each other many times and, thankfully, we're good. But we both live with the scars drowning people carry.

Not long after that abominable *Washington Post* statement, someone saw me drowning and threw me something to hang onto. In the wake of everything blowing up in my life, I received a lot of notes from people, most of which would fall somewhere on the spectrum of "encouragement." I tried to respond to them because I was grateful; I really was. One of those "I'm praying for you" notes came from a woman named Stacie. I had no idea who she was, had never met her or engaged with her on social media, nothing. Until she said something, I didn't know she existed. But she commented (her first ever on Twitter) on one of my tweets. I responded with "Thank you," and she commented again with something like—"I know what you're going through."

> In return, Giovanni told me that empathizing Italians say *L'ho provato sulla mia pelle*, which means "I have experienced that on my own skin." Meaning, I have also been burned or scarred in this way, and I know exactly what you're going through.
>
> —Elizabeth Gilbert, *Eat, Pray, Love*

Stacie's not Italian; she's 100% Texan, but she essentially said, "I have experienced that on my own skin." Her words were buoyant. She threw them from a safe distance (Texas). And they got my attention. I reached for those words and held on, not knowing just how much of a lifeline Stacie would be.

Part 2
THE LOST HEART

Chapter 4
THAT SAD, SAD, COUNTRY

Divorce has many witnesses, many victims. It is a lurid duet that entices observers to the dance; the *pas de deux* expands, flowers into a monstrous choreography and draws in friends, children and relatives. Each divorce is the death of a small civilization. Two people declare war on each other, and their screams and tears and days of withdrawal infect their entire world with the bacilli of their pain. There are no clean divorces. Divorces should be conducted in abattoirs, surgical wards, blood banks or funeral homes. The greatest fury comes from the wound where love once issued forth.

—Pat Conroy, "Anatomy of a Divorce," *Atlanta Magazine*, November 1, 1978

P at Conroy's account of his divorce is incredibly sad, incredibly well-written, and incredibly true. About midway through his account, Conroy mentions "the children":

There are no metaphors powerful enough to describe the moment when you tell the children about the divorce. Divorces without children are minor-league divorces. To look into the eyes of your children and to tell them that you are mutilating their family, that you are changing the structure of their world by a process of radical surgery that will make all their tomorrows different is an act of desperate courage that I never want to repeat in my life. When I talk to people about their divorces, the children are the subject that produces the heaviest sorrow.[21]

The heaviest sorrow? Yes, yes, it is.

It was acutely clear to me that my professional life was over—no more influential pastor, no more sought-after conference speaker, no more best-selling author, no more rising star rising. And then it was equally clear that my personal life was over—no more marriage, no more life as I'd known it for twenty-one years. It was, as Conroy wrote, the death of our small civilization.

Was it home where we were standing? Was it memories burnt down to nothing? Then watch this empire fall down.

—Le Youth

STAYED AND STRAYED

The conventional way of thinking around adultery is that if a man has an affair, it's because he's looking for a physical connection—in other words, sex. On the other hand, if a woman has an affair, it's because she's looking for something more emotional. That's conventional thinking, rather binary, and in my opinion dangerously naive because that's not the way it was with me. I wasn't looking for sex. As I said earlier, that reconnection with my girlfriend from high school opened up something in me, and that something didn't have anything to do with filling some physical void. Something deeply emotional, even something romantic, was stirred in me that seemed to me missing at that time in my marriage.

Kim and I met when we were both nineteen years old, and let's just say we were wild. But by the time we were twenty-one years old, through a variety of circumstances, God got a hold of both of us and life changed rather dramatically. We stopped living the way we had been living and started moving together in a totally different direction—toward God. We decided soon after that to get engaged, and it was during our engagement that we found out we were expecting our first child. We were kids, just kids.

So, marriage didn't start light and easy for us. But in time we settled in and began building a life together. The first seven years we were married, I was in school—four years of college and three years of seminary. In that time, we had all three of our children, moved a total of five times, and lived in three different states. Yeah, do the math. Life was exciting, but exhausting. As the years went on and life got even busier, some things were left behind or got lost, I'm not sure which. Probably some mixture of both. Our marriage wasn't easy (what marriage is?), but it also wasn't bad. Because we basically grew up together, we had a lot of shared experiences, a lot of happy history. In many ways, we had a fun marriage. She was my best friend. And I was hers. We laughed a lot. We made a lot of really great memories. And we raised three amazing kids that we're both extremely proud of. Our life together was full and rich. But over the course of time and compounded by the complexities of life, gaps developed in some key places. Either we moved away from each other in those places or were never connected in them to begin with. Some things were taken for granted, while other things were neglected. None of this happened intentionally; most of it happened unconsciously, and all of it happened gradually. But it happened.

It's difficult trying to make any sense of what happened in my first marriage. In the quest for understanding, there's always the temptation to reduce it down to some mathematical equation— *my-always-wanting MORE* + *just-kids-having-kids+GAPS* = the unmaking of a marriage. But that's not fair to either my ex-wife or me or this thing called "marriage." It's simply and always more complicated than that. I never want to minimize my part in all of it, yet when people speak of such things in simplistic terms, like "connecting the dots" or something, I believe it shows they just don't know, or they haven't been there. None of this means I don't pay attention to the stories of others who have walked similar paths, sifting through other screwups looking for clues or something beyond "it just happened"—even if it did. Because I do.

A Burning in My Bones is the authorized biography of Eugene Peterson written by Winn Collier. While my grandfather was known as America's pastor, Peterson was best known as "the pastor," best-selling author of *The Message*, and buddy of Bono. Far too much attention has been placed on a series of unfortunate events near the end of Peterson's life, and Collier's biography is a remedy to that, for it tells the whole story of a man's life, not just his final interview. One aspect of the biography is an endearing portrait of Eugene's marriage to his wife, Jan. But even their marriage ran aground on some of what I'm trying to describe about mine. No, I'm not saying it was the same, but I am saying it's not entirely different. There was a woman who fell in love with Eugene Peterson, a woman who was not his wife. Collier leads into the story by saying:

> Getting a handle on the layers of this second pastoral relationship is knotty, especially in our voyeuristic culture, where everything between women

and men is immediately framed by questions of sexual intimacies. We have little space for relational layers and complexities, the many-angled dimensions related to being in proximity and relationship with another human. Either we run roughshod over propriety and boundaries or we become prudish and act as if emotions, and even attractions, are something to deny with puritanical terror.[22]

The reality was the Petersons were in a challenging season of their marriage and ministry. He was fifty-seven at the time (that's right—*fifty-seven*) and along comes a woman who sought Eugene out for spiritual direction. In contrast to some of the indolent people in his congregation, he found her energy and passion and hunger for God a delight. His journals indicate: "I catch this wild wind of beauty and grace coming off her . . ." Longer story short, Peterson realized the dangers of this relationship and cut things off, entirely. He returned to his wife Jan. Again, from his journals, he shares that "there is a deep fear in my psyche that makes me vulnerable to such ventures onto thin ice . . ." but there was "the gracious rescue."

I share this story, not because his and mine are identical; they aren't. I share it because even someone as seemingly solid as Eugene Peterson knew of the thin ice; he was acutely aware of his vulnerabilities as a flesh-and-blooder. And his attraction to this woman didn't have anything to do with a deficit in his physical, sexual self. It was something beyond that. But he stopped and got off the ice. I, on the other hand, didn't. I continued to skate, and the ice gave way beneath me.

Cheryl Strayed holds a place in the memoir revival close to Mary Karr's. Her 2012 memoir *Wild* reached No. 1 on the *New York Times* Best Seller list. Dwight Garner of the *New York Times* described *Wild* as "uplifting, but not in the way of many memoirs, where the uplift makes you feel that you're committing mental suicide."[23] Before her acclaim for *Wild*, Strayed was best-known (although anonymously) for the online advice column at The Rumpus website, "Dear Sugar." The range of letters Strayed received is amazing. She compiled some of them in her blisteringly honest book *Tiny Beautiful Things: Advice on Love and Life.*

In the chapter titled "A Bit of Sully in Your Sweet," Strayed responds to a twenty-nine-year-old woman engaged to be married who is wrestling with the reality of infidelity she has witnessed in her sister's marriage—a marriage she had believed was the perfect marriage. She's scared. She wants healthy love. She's asking for the secret to a good marriage, a happy-ever-after match. This portion of Strayed's response stood out to me, where she encourages thinking deeply about "the moment a transgression occurs":

> This will require a rethink about your own dark capacities, as well as those of your future husband, and the members of various couples you admire. Most people don't cheat because they're cheaters. They cheat because they are people. They are driven by hunger or for the experience of someone being hungry once more for them. They find themselves in friendships that take an unintended turn or they seek them out because they're horny or drunk or damaged from all the stuff they didn't get when they were kids. There is love. There is lust. There is opportunity. There is alcohol. And youth. There is loneliness and boredom and sorrow and weakness and self-destruction and idiocy and arrogance and romance and ego and nostalgia and power and need. There is the compelling

temptation of intimacies with someone other than the person with whom one is most intimate. Which is a complicated way of saying, it's a long damn life, Happily Ever After. And people get mucked up in it from time to time. Even the people we marry. Even us . . . [24]

We all live and move and have our being within a complex framework of fallenness. What I mean is that we are all broken people living in a broken world with other broken people. Or, as Eugene Peterson puts it in his translation of Jeremiah 17:9, *"The heart is dark and deceitful, a puzzle no one can figure out"* (MSG). Knowing this doesn't take away the pain or sadness from any of it, but it does frame it, gives it a border if you will, so it isn't so large that it destroys us.

People get mucked up. Kim and I did. People screw up. I did.

It happens.

THAT SAD, DARK COUNTRY

Each divorce has its own natural metaphors that organically grow out of the special circumstances of the dying marriage. The metaphors assume many shapes, some unthreatening, some ludicrous, some hilarious and some phantasmagoric, all final. They come to represent the end of the thing, the last acting out of the ceremony of amputation.

—Pat Conroy

I filed for divorce on August 20, 2015, two weeks before I moved to Orlando. My divorce was final in February 2016. The distance from Orlando to Fort Lauderdale is 212 miles. For the five months until my divorce was final, although I was only three hours and some change in distance from the world I'd known, I was in another country. But by then I'd been an exile for quite some time.

In *Amazing Grace*, Kathleen Norris writes about an important breakthrough in regard to belief that came when she "learned to be as consciously skeptical and questioning of my disbelief and my doubts as I was of my burgeoning faith."[25] At the time she found an ally in Fr. Martin Smith, an Anglican monk, who wrote that "ambivalence is a sacred emotion." Smith said that he finds "a widespread need in contemporary spirituality to find ways of praying and engaging with God, our selves, and one another that have room for simultaneous contradictions, the experience of opposite emotions. We need to find the sacredness in living the tensions . . ."[26]

That perfectly articulates what I was going through at the time—*ambivalence*. In the wake of my self-implosion, I was living in a combustible dust of consequences. I was scared, ashamed, angry, hurt, embarrassed, confused. I was walking in circles, backwards. I didn't know who I was. Or where I was. I couldn't make sense of what I had done, who I had become, and who others had become as well. I felt like a stranger to myself and to those I knew. I didn't know what to do next. I felt everything and nothing at the same time. I wish someone, anyone, would have said something like, "Tullian, this ambivalence, man, it's sacred. It may not feel like it, but it is. Trust it as such."

So, let me say that to you now. If you're in such a season of life where you're nothing but a bundle of contradictions, that's sacred. In other words, God is right there, which on a mental level some of us would say *okay sure*, but at a gut level, it rarely feels that way. "Stick with that" is something my friend and counselor Paul Zahl would say to me each time I would feverishly pour out my fear and sadness, my hopelessness, heartbreak, confusion, and rage during that season. His point was that there's a lot to learn about yourself and a lot to see of God in the ruins of life—in the middle of hard things, bad things, painful things—so don't be too quick to look for an exit. Stick with it because ambivalence is a sacred emotion. Fr. Martin Smith adds: "There is much at stake when belief and doubt go into the crucible; despair might emerge. But with luck, faith and hope appear."[27]

"Ambivalence is a sacred emotion" is something you would expect an Anglican monk to say. My take on it would be—it's okay to be a confused exile. And was I ever. I did come across a phrase in French—*Entre Chien et Loup*—which means "between dog and wolf." That phrase describes that time of day when the light makes it difficult to distinguish between a dog and a wolf, friend and foe, known and unknown. In a figurative sense of that time, we can't always know whether we're safe or threatened; we feel our eyes deceive us, and we question everything we think we know. In the weeks and months that followed, I spent all my time sacredly ambivalent, confused, exiled, breech between the dog and the wolf. I say breech because something was trying to be born there. I didn't know that then and would have bristled at the thought, but looking back now, I can see it, feel it. Something was struggling to be born in that ambivalent season. Something I now name *freedom*.

In my exile, there was Stacie.

That's right, Stacie. After that initial Twitter exchange in early July 2015, Stacie and I exchanged phone numbers and continued to communicate via text. Crazy, I know, but we did. We then talked on the phone—she shared her story; I shared mine. Stacie had been married twice but had been single for a few years by the time we started talking. Needless to say, she'd gone through some difficult seasons of heartache and heartbreak. I still had hopes, albeit slim, of salvaging my first marriage, and that was some of what Stacie and I talked about in those early conversations. Yes, I was having conversations about my first wife with another woman who I'd never met in person in the immediate wreckage of my first marriage which I thought I might still be able to "save."

And because some part of me did want to try to save my marriage, after only about a week of conversations with Stacie, I told her we needed to stop talking, that I had to focus, and as much as I appreciated our conversations, they were muddying the water for me. Over the next weeks, however, there were some significant developments, which made it painfully clear that my first marriage wasn't going to make it. Trust across the board had evaporated. There was too much water under the bridge. And it was in the wake of that realization that I noticed something. I missed talking to Stacie. So, I sent Stacie a text message. Then I called her. And on that call, I invited her to come to Fort Lauderdale so we could meet. She said, "When?" And I said, "How about tomorrow?" She thought I was kidding. I wasn't. She said, "Okay." Again, I realize how off the charts insane this sounds because it was. Crazy. Stupid. Reckless. Unwise. Adulterous, even. All the above. But Stacie flew down, and we sat on the beach for a couple of days. We talked, I showed her some of my favorite spots, we listened to some good music, and we ate some good food. When Stacie left to go back to Texas, I had no idea what my future held, but I could faintly see her in it.

There were two things of note initially about Stacie—the first was her empathetic response ("I know what you're going through") and the second was that I had a sense she was safe. I was bunkered in a hotel room at the time, hiding out. I didn't know who to trust beyond a handful of people. In my corner of the world, my "fall from grace" as the headlines read, was the talk of the town. Reporters and basement bloggers saw blood in the water, and they were constantly circling.

I wasn't surprised by that, but I also was. I understand that Christian celebrity + famous family + famous church + "sexual" sin = juicy story. I get that. But I was never one of those preachers who said, "I'm a good guy. Follow me." Quite the opposite. I was well known for talking about my own messed-upness, sharing openly about my own brokenness. I never pretended to have it all together. In fact, one of the reasons people listened to my messages and read my books is that I was candid about my own ongoing need for God's grace. I was known (and appreciated) for saying things like: "God loves screwed-up people because screwed-up people are all that there are."

But here's what I learned during that time: we like our leaders to admit screwed-upness in theory. But screwed-upness in practice? That's a different animal. I've noticed, for instance, that people love it when leaders say they are fallen and broken just like the rest of us, until that leader does something that the rest of us fallen and broken people do. When that happens, the love and admiration quickly evaporate and are replaced by disgust and disillusionment, and all too often, social expulsion. Exile.

In my exile, there was Stacie—someone who was not-Florida, someone not-church-related, someone unaffected by the explosion I caused. She seemed sane, someone who'd been through the fire. She was coming out of a losing season; I was diving into one. She knew what it felt like to be a loser, which Wendell Berry defines as "somebody whom nobody knows what to do with." A loser—that's what I was too. I guess what I'm saying is Stacie was a friend to me. Right off the bat I trusted her, and that was not a slight thing. Still isn't.

> We love those who know the worst about us and don't turn their faces away.
>
> —Walker Percy, *Love in the Ruins*

Over the last several years, I've said to many people that true friends are revealed when you're at your worst, not your best—when you're at the bottom, not the top. When you're at the top, it's hard to know who your real friends are because you have so much to offer. Everyone loves a winner. They all want a piece. But when you're at the bottom? When you have nothing to offer but leprosy and liability to anyone who comes close? Well, that's when you take notice of who is there, who has not turned their face away.

Apart from Stacie and my three kids, no one, and I mean no one, personified "true friend" to me more during that time than Paul Zahl.

Paul and I got to know each other years ago after I reached out to him to express my appreciation for his excellent book *Grace in Practice: A Theology of Everyday Life*. At that time, my career was taking off, and Paul's was slowing down. He had recently retired from a lifetime of faithful and fruitful service in the ministry as a pastor, seminary president, scholar, counselor, and author. From his many prestigious posts, Paul's unwavering commitment to brilliantly articulating the radicality of God's grace often got him into trouble with all the right people. As evidence, I present this quote of his:

> Grace is love that has nothing to do with you, the beloved. It has everything to do with the lover. Grace is irrational in that it has nothing to do with weights and measures. It has nothing to do with my intrinsic qualities or so-called "gifts" (whatever they may be). It reflects a decision on the part of the giver, the one who loves, in relation to the receiver, the one who is loved, that negates any qualifications the receiver may personally hold . . . . Grace is one-way love. Take an inventory of yourself. Watch other people about whose

happiness you care. You will see it over and over: one-way love lifts up. One-way love cures. One-way love transforms. It is the change agent of life.[28]

From the moment we met, I knew I had made a friend. Over the years, Paul became a pastor to me—a counselor, a mentor, a sounding board, a real father figure. He took a keen interest in my work, but more importantly, he took a keen interest in me. He wholeheartedly believed the message that he had lived for (and, in many ways, died for), and it showed in his friendship to me.

So, it shouldn't have been a surprise to me that when I set my life on fire, Paul was one of the first people to rush in. When you are living with a secret and it finally gets exposed, you want to run and hide. You understand that everybody in your life will be rightfully angry and hurt because they've been betrayed in some way and therefore want nothing to do with you, at least for a time. So, I naturally assumed Paul would feel that way too, especially since he had invested so much in me. And I'm sure he did—he had every right to. But as people were running away from me, Paul was running toward me, *toward* the flames.

In my exile, there was Stacie, and there was Paul. Beacons in that sad, dark country.

Chapter 5
LOST BETWEEN TWO SHORES

We have met the enemy, and he is us.

—Pogo

Y ou would think that after all the damage my adultery caused to myself and others, I would've fallen down to my knees in heartfelt remorse. But I didn't. Well, I did . . . but I also didn't. I was feeling sorry for my sin (especially the way it hurt people I love) but I was also feeling sorry for myself. As is often the case when we get caught, things get worse before they start to get better. Rather than stopping to assess the damage and take responsibility for it, for some reason we double down, or at least I did. For me, the embarrassing truth is that for a while afterward, I frantically wandered in the wasteland of selfishness that I'd chosen to inhabit. Rather than blaming myself first for all the hurt I caused, I pointed fingers in every direction, including heavenward. I was angry at God and others and doing everything I could to save myself from the wreckage I caused. I was in full self-salvation mode. I was withholding the truth from people (for example, my friend Paul) and spinning the narrative in my favor at every turn, frenetically trying to manage my image and minimize my own culpability. Everything I did to try to salvage what I could and fill the gaping voids created by my own screwups caused even more harm to myself and others. Even in exile, I was still on the run. I was still hiding. I was spiraling—getting worse, not better.

I write now, many years later, with the gift of perspective, from a distance, trying to reflect and make some sense of what was going on in my life. As best I can tell, I was operating in a state of shock—not just shock at what was happening around me and happening to me, but mostly shock at what was happening in me and coming out of me with such spontaneity: rage, rationalization, self-pity, thirst for revenge, suicidal thoughts, deceitfulness, a sense of entitlement. And it was coming out of me like it had been there all along, which, of course, it had been. You yourself might be appallingly surprised at what kind of nastiness you're capable of given the right set of circumstances. I know I was. Now maybe it shouldn't have shocked me that I could be so foul with such instinctive ease. After all, I had a low anthropology. So, I knew I was bad. What I didn't know until that season, however, was just how large my capacity for badness actually is. Far from self-hatred, I was coming into a self-knowledge I'd only experienced in part up to that point in my life.

Here's how I see it now.

In one of his final interviews before his untimely death, the poet John O'Donohue talked to "On Being" host Krista Tippett about how in this country (America) we've reduced identity to biography—I am where I came from, what's happened to me, etc. So, if I tell you my story, I've shared my identity with you. But O'Donohue cautioned that identity and biography are not the same thing, far from it.[29] Identity is far, far more complex. For the most part, what I had experienced up to that point in my life was a biographical sense of my badness (what I'd done or failed to do)—I knew I'd done wrong or that I routinely failed to do right, and I was able to talk about that, write about that, share about that. But my avalanche of embarrassing, destructive behavior, all at once and with relative ease? That revealed to me something deeper, far more complex than biographical badness. That revealed something about my heart.

What I was experiencing was the difference between generalities and specifics. In his book *The Autobiography of Mark Rutherford*, William Hale White describes Mr. Rutherford's childhood pastor, Brother Holderness, and his willingness to confess publicly that he was a sinner, a broken man just like everybody else. But, White says, if the pastor would have confessed one *actual* indiscretion, he "would have been visited by suspension or expulsion."[30]

I believe White makes a profound point: it is one thing to admit that you're a sinner; it is another thing altogether to admit your sins. With a wave of my arm I can say, "I know I'm not perfect. I'm a sinner and I'm not as good as I should be. I screw up and do things I shouldn't"—and for some reason, I can swallow that, as can the people listening. That's emotionally digestible for me, and for them. But it's a completely different thing to admit that "I'm lying," "I'm selfish," "I've been keeping secrets from those closest to me," or "I've been unfaithful to those primary people I promised my fidelity to." To not only say but to see that we are blind, resentful, vindictive, irrational, greedy, prideful, unforgiving, lustful, and instinctively self-righteous? That's like a bone in the throat. Learning *that* about ourselves only comes through suffering, crashing and burning, bottoming out, and running out of our own steam. It takes being exposed—a real confrontation with ourselves, which we fight to avoid, delay, and push back at all costs. As one of my counselors told me early on, circumstances don't create the condition of the heart. Rather, circumstances reveal the condition of the heart. And what was revealed to me about my heart in the wake of personal collapse was sobering. I have seen the enemy, and it is me.

DEATH OF THE DREAM

> For sale: baby shoes, never worn.
>
> —Attributed to Ernest Hemingway

Legend has it that sometime in the 1920s, Ernest Hemingway sat in a hotel (probably the Algonquin) with his writer friends and bet them he could write a story with a full narrative in just six words. Money was placed on the table; Hemingway jotted down his six words on a napkin, and the rest is literary history except there's no evidence that this scene ever happened, none. In some sense it's become one of those "well if it isn't true, it oughta be" stories, and the six-word story approach birthed what is popularly known as "flash fiction."

If challenged to write a six-word story to describe my life from the summer of 2015 through the end of that year, here's my attempt: One man, two-bedroom apartment rental.

Sure, it pales in comparison to Hemingway's, but those six words speak volumes about my story at the time. In fact, they reveal what Pat Conroy called the natural metaphor each divorce has, which represents "the end of the thing, the last acting out of the ceremony of amputation."[31] When I walked up the stairs to that rented two-bedroom apartment in Orlando, opened the door, and stepped into an empty unfurnished shell that could house anyone or anything for a period of time, I knew "the end of the thing." As I've mentioned before, Kim and I had purchased a house, gutted it, and turned it into a home with all the personal touches so it fit us. It was the home I thought I'd die in, seriously. And I guess I did. The stark contrast between the warmth and familiarity of that home and the cold, sterile reality of that apartment ushered in a sadness I'd never experienced before. It was the death of my marriage, yes, and also the death of the dream. I say "the dream" because I'm a romantic at heart, and the picture of hearth and home and family runs deep in me. I'm the guy who dreamed of reaching eighty years old and sitting on the beach with Kim, the wife of my youth, surrounded by our kids and grandkids and with me grabbing her wrinkled hand with my wrinkled hand and saying, with a satisfied and grateful smile, "We made it. There were days when I wasn't sure, but we endured. We made it. I loved you then. I love you even more now."

That sentimental dream meant a great deal to me. Still does. Now, did I rip that picture to shreds and blow up any chance of living that scene on a beach as an octogenarian? I did. And as a result, I consigned myself to the lifelong ache of an unfinished love story, a haunting "what-if?" Now, if you live in some Thomas Kinkaid world where everything's clean and brightly pastel-colored and there are the purely innocent and the purely guilty, then you'd say it served me right; I got what I deserved. And that is true. But I would plead with you to consider the unbearable sadness that even the guilty carry, for it was not just any dream that died, but *the* dream, the one I believe every human holds in some form in their heart—the dream of home.

In this excerpt from *Sex, Economy, Freedom & Community*, Wendell Berry aptly captures key aspects of what "home" means to most of us:

> No settled family or community has ever called its
> home place an "environment." None has ever called its

feeling for its home place "biocentric" or "anthropocentric." None has ever thought of its connection to its home place as "ecological," deep or shallow. The concepts and insights of the ecologists are of great usefulness in our predicament, and we can hardly escape the need to speak of "ecology" and "ecosystems." But the terms themselves are culturally sterile. They come from the juiceless, abstract intellectuality of the universities which was invented to disconnect, displace, and disembody the mind. The real names of the environment are the names of rivers and river valleys; creeks, ridges, and mountains; towns and cities; lakes, woodlands, lanes roads, creatures, and people.[32]

One man, two-bedroom apartment rental. Disconnected. Displaced. Disembodied.

I left *home*—the one on Barton Road in the Hillsboro Shores neighborhood just north of Fort Lauderdale, Florida, my dream neighborhood with its own beach. The *home* where Kim and Genna and Nate and Gabe lived. And once upon a time, me.

THE MOTH GOD

> like a moth you eat away all that is dear to us . . .
>
> —Psalm 39:12 Book of Common Prayer

A friend asked me once if I could point to lessons I've learned after having gone through all the things I'm telling you about in this book. I paused a minute because my mind doesn't really work in the "four lessons learned" mode. In fact, I typically rebel against that type of formulaic self-reflection. But after that minute, I said this: "I've learned self-awareness. I thought I was self-aware, and to some degree I was. But, man, I had no idea."

In 2011, I wrote a book titled *Jesus + Nothing = Everything*. The beginning of that book recounts the struggles I experienced in becoming the pastor of Coral Ridge Presbyterian and the challenge of merging that historic, very established megachurch with a not-historic church I had started just five years earlier.[33] From a leadership standpoint, things got hard, really hard. Some people didn't like the decisions I was making or the sermons I was preaching. They just didn't like me because I was different from their previous pastor. Well, this was a first for me. Wherever I'd been and whatever I'd done up until that point was widely accepted and almost always appreciated. I had been loved wherever I went. But that had changed. In the middle of that bruhaha, I started to realize how much of my identity had been grounded in the acceptance and love of other people. So, without that acceptance, I struggled to know who I was, and I found myself telling God I wanted my old life back. Essentially, I wanted out. But God made it clear that it wasn't my old life I wanted back; it was my old idols I wanted back, and that he loved me too much to give them back.

When I wrote *Jesus + Nothing = Everything* in 2011, do you want to know who I wrote it for? The 2015-Me—that's right, future me. Sound crazy? What I know now that I didn't know then is that my implosion had been building for a few years, gathering steam. A subtle shift had come on like the slow creep of the tide rather than a sudden tidal wave, a shift in identity—from locating my identity in God's love for me to locating my identity in what I was making of myself—my accomplishments, my accolades, my success.

In other words, my worth, my value, my deepest sense of who I was and what made me matter—my identity—was anchored in my status, my reputation, my position, who my friends were, my skill at communicating, my ability to lead, the praise I received, the opportunities I had, financial security, and so on. Basically, the way the world has and always will measure worth. And because of this, my losses did not simply usher in grief and pain and shame and regret. They ushered in a crippling identity crisis. We typically don't know what it is we depend on to make life worth living until we lose it. Without the things I had come to depend on to make me feel valuable and important, I no longer knew who I was. It wasn't just that I lost everything—I lost myself. I was learning the painful way that attaching our identity to our activity will put us on a roller coaster of misery because we spend all our time working toward an identity rather than from one.

When I was at my absolute worst and most desperate, my friend Paul Zahl said something to me that I will never forget: "Tullian, the purpose behind the suffering you are going through is to kick you into a new freedom from false definitions of who you are." I did not understand the depths of Paul's statement in that moment; there was no way I could have. But I've learned. And I'm learning.

> You must learn one thing. The world was made to be free in.
>
> —David Whyte, "Sweet Darkness"

God, as it turns out, is *still* setting me free from false definitions of who I am. Despite my intense efforts to resist, he is still kicking me into new vistas of freedom from my romanticized notions of who I used to be defined by the life I used to have. So far, he hasn't shown any signs of backing off his loving mission to set this stubbornly sentimental captive free.

Think, for a minute, about the spirit of the age in which we currently live—the attention economy. As author Mark Manson (*The Subtle Art of Not Giving a F*ck*) describes it: "one constant, never-ending stream of non sequiturs and self-referential garbage that passes in through our eyes and out of our brains at the speed of a touchscreen."[34] On any given day, most of that energy/time/money is laser-focused on grabbing and keeping our attention revolves around *identity*—you and I finding, let's say, our authentic self, the real me, unencumbered by _____ (fill in the blank with our individual and/or collective oppressor(s)), or you and I finding our authentic group or tribe, the real we. And most days it's a one-two punch of both, all with the goal of adding (or sometimes subtracting) something from our lives that will accurately identify us.

There's nothing wrong with finding out who you are and who your people are. That's been going on since the world started turning. But since that beginning, God's "infinitely tender hand" has been at work for our freedom, so that whether we succeed in catching what we're chasing—our preferred political party wins or we finally discover the world's greatest T-shirt or our diet is in accordance with our primal ancestors—you and I have already been caught. By God. And we can say: "I'm the one God loves." That's our identity.

I told a friend recently that now when I see someone having their identity knocked out from underneath them, I don't want to avoid them or chide them, I want to give 'em a hug. Because having everything you hold dear eaten away from you, that's like open heart surgery without anesthesia. It hurts.

3-PS: MY ALLITERATIVE IDENTITY

Professional.

Personal.

Publican.

When Kevin Labby and Willow Creek Presbyterian Church reached out to me, it was in an effort to help me get back on track *professionally*. As I already mentioned, Kevin invited me to join Willow Creek in an administrative role—to ensure health insurance, plus provide me a chance to go to counseling. But the bottom line for me? Time to figure out next steps *professionally*, to salvage that **P** of my identity.

After I resigned from Coral Ridge for "moral failure" and was subsequently defrocked by the Presbytery, LIBERATE (the conference and media ministry I'd started in 2011), the book deals, the speaking engagements, the travel opportunities, all my professional cred—that all vanished almost overnight. The very day I resigned, Coral Ridge shut down LIBERATE and removed all my content from their platforms. Every sermon I'd preached and every article I'd written for the previous six years—all gone, gone with the wind. All twelve of my speaking engagements that had been lined up for the fall of 2015? Gone, every one of them canceled in the span of 24 hours. I exaggerate not. All my books were almost immediately removed from Christian bookstores. I had just signed a hefty book deal and although the publisher was gracious to work with me on *something* in the future, the "hefty" went away. So, part of what Kevin and I started working on soon after I got to Willow Creek was resurrecting LIBERATE. Kevin was the one leading that charge, but that behind-the-scenes effort is what got me up on those dark mornings in that lonely Orlando apartment. It gave me some purpose for living. Maybe that would be the canopy under which new books and new speaking and new conferences and new opportunities could sprout. Maybe some of what was lost professionally could be found again. Maybe.

While my final affair was very public, only a handful of people were aware of the one in 2014 that I told you about. What the public knew about was one affair. And, most understood that these things happen with people all the time and that pastors are people too. So as the weeks rolled by in the summer and fall of 2015, there was still a lot of public support for me. Many people were sad, some were shocked, and still others were angry. But the vast majority were gracious, forgiving, and sympathetic. Yet as I've said before and I'll say it again, sin finds you.

My time at Willow Creek was supposed to last one year, but it came to a sudden end after seven months when, in the early spring of 2016, the 2014 affair I wrote about earlier became public knowledge. I'd gotten wind of the fact that it was most likely going to come out a few days before it did, and so I met with Kevin Labby and said, "I need to tell you something. You have to know about this. It happened a year before the other, and it was dealt with; you can talk to any of the guys who were a part of that process, but I think it's going public soon, and you need to know." His response was gracious, something along the lines of, "Thank you for telling me. You didn't have to. After all, it happened long before you came here; it was dealt with then, and you've done everything we've asked you to do while here." I breathed a sigh.

A few days later, that affair did indeed become public knowledge. Not only did the initial public support for me dry up immediately, but the leadership at Willow Creek severed all ties with me abruptly, which is not what I was led to believe would happen. But that's what happened. My "things" were boxed up and taken to the curb, literally. Professional identity? Game over.

There were others too, first responders from the GRACE BRIGADE I'll call them, friends who rushed to my car wreck, so to speak, but bailed when the authorities discovered bodies in the trunk, so to speak. The heat just got too hot. I get it, but it still hurt. I learned the hard way that not all friends are friends, and that grace on paper and grace in practice are two very, very different things. Yet there was an exception, at least one. I'll never forget the text I received at the time from Paul Zahl: "I just want you to know, dear Tullian, I'm still here." Grace in practice.

> There must be at least one
> on this earth who preserves
> the idea, one impractical fool
> who will not bend the knee but
> chooses to turn the cheek.
> There must be at least one
> on this bruised plain who wears
> the look of rightness, a long-sufferer
> who knows the wounds men make
> do not quickly heal.
> There must be at least one
> in this shadowed valley
> who will cede life for a friend,
> a willed renunciator of
> the present in favor of a future.
> There must be at least one
> with no commercial value,
> whose very life reminds us of our
> lovely and terrible birthright,
> one who longs for the appearing.
>
> —John Blase, "At Least One"

With my professional identity kaput, I shifted my energies to trying to restore some shred of my personal identity, to recover some of my familiar, all while spending more and more time with the woman who left Texas and moved to Orlando to be near me—Stacie. Yes, you read that right. A month after I moved to Orlando, Stacie left her beloved Lone Star state and rented a house not far from me, so we could be closer to one another and figure out whether there was anything beyond our initial attraction. You might think my life at the time was this chessboard, full of figures making both surprising and not-so-surprising moves. Chessboard, I wish—that would have held the unlikely but at least slim possibility of winning. But my life was 52-card pickup—someone (me) had carelessly but with intention thrown the entire deck in the air, scattering the cards as farmers used to say, from hell to breakfast. Stacie offered to help me try to find my cards, any cards, one card even. Winning was never an option. I was just trying to survive.

What follows in the chapters ahead is the painful unraveling of my personal identity, some of which was already happening, some of which would fully come in time. It all left me in a scary place, that third **P** of identity—publican. I didn't even have the presence of mind to lift my eyes much less my head. I think I prayed "Lord, have mercy on me, a sinner." I think I did, but I'm not sure. I may have just said, "Mercy."

> But the publican, standing afar off, would not lift up so much as his eyes unto heaven, but smote his breast, saying, God, be thou merciful to me a sinner.
>
> —Luke18:13 ASV

Chapter 6
BOTH SIDES NOW

It's full of flowers and heart-shaped boxes
And things we're all too young to know

—Peter Gabriel, "The Book of Love"

Stacie and I met on the other side of failure and loss, which is a vastly different place than the side where things are new and fresh and young and untested—"full of flowers and heart-shaped boxes." We've seen both sides now. It's not that one side is better than the other, that's not what I'm saying at all. I'm saying they're different. And if you know, you know.

If you love someone, set them free.
If they come back they're yours;
if they don't they never were.

—Richard Bach

"Trust God with this." That's what Stacie heard from Mary, as in Mary Zahl, wife of my good friend Paul Zahl. Paul and Mary, in

addition to my mother and kids, were the first people I introduced
Stacie to. I had moved to Orlando in September 2015, and about a
month later Stacie moved there as well. She rented a house near my
apartment and found a job; we began dating very discreetly, and I
gradually introduced her to my closest friends. Almost a year later,
August 2016, in Houston, Texas, thirteen people witnessed Stacie
and me exchange wedding vows. I wish I could tell you those months
in between that led up to "I do" were a whirlwind fairy tale. I wish I
could. A whirlwind? You bet. A fairy tale? Not a chance, unless you
count Grimm's. That's why at one point Mary told Stacie, "Trust
God with this."

ALL THE THINGS

> Here is what I learned once I began studying whooping cranes: only
> a small part of studying them has anything to do with the birds.
> Instead we counted berries. Counted crabs. Measured water salinity.
> Stood in the mud. Measured the speed of the wind.
> It turns out, if you want to save a species, you don't spend your time
> staring at the bird you want to save. You look at the things it relies
> on to live instead. You ask if there is enough to eat and drink. You
> ask if there is a safe place to sleep. Is there enough here to survive?
>
> —C J Hauser, *The Crane Wife*

All the things. All the things I'd relied on to live. That's what I
lost, and was losing. One of those "things," as odd as it may sound,
was my religion. Losing that thing changed me, for the better.
Willow Creek hosted a conference on Presidents Day weekend in
February 2016. That was the same weekend that we had held the
LIBERATE conference each year from 2011 to 2015. Remember,

LIBERATE shut down when I resigned from Coral Ridge. The LIBERATE conference had been a rallying point, a gathering spot, for thousands of people from all over the world who traveled to Fort Lauderdale once a year because they craved the message of grace that we were devoted to delivering. And now it was gone. There were many who clamored for something similar, so the plan was to get some version of the LIBERATE conference back up and running by 2017.

The 2016 conference at Willow Creek was supposed to be a placeholder conference until LIBERATE came back the following year. The same speakers that I used to bring in for LIBERATE were brought in for this conference. And while it was wisely decided that I would not be a main speaker (too soon, bad optics), the organizers wanted me to use my influence to promote the conference and be visibly present, so I agreed to sit on a panel with the speakers (all close friends of mine at the time) and have a theological discussion about grace and its related subjects. I'd honestly looked forward to the experience, having the opportunity to speak in a public setting once again while surrounded by people who knew me, people who were my allies.

But while they knew me, they also didn't. They didn't have a clue as to how desperate I felt on the stage that day. Surrounded by people, all eyes on me, but feeling totally alone. I was putting on a brave face, one of those simply-to-Thy-cross-I'll-cling faces, but it was nothing more than a facade. My divorce had just been finalized. My family was irreparably broken. I missed the wife of my youth. I missed my kids. I missed our family the way it had been for two decades. I missed the life we'd had together, the life I'd taken for granted, the full life that I'd squandered. I felt internally and externally shipwrecked. I didn't have the strength to cling to anything, and some days that included the desire to keep on. You wouldn't believe the number of suicidal thoughts I'd had, something I would have never believed I could even entertain. But I did. Almost daily. Yet there I was, on a spotlit stage, to *talk* about grace.

The moment that stands out in my memory happened in the middle of a very robust academic discussion on that panel where big words like *sanctification* and *justification* and *imputation* filled the stage, important words that I very much believe in then and now. I had facilitated discussions like this and thrived in them many times before. I'd always felt at home on a stage having a theological conversation like the one we were having that day. But as scholarly words and phrases, coupled with confident erudition, danced in the conference air, I had only four words in my head: *Who the hell cares?* For me, this intellectual dissection of God's unmerited favor fell flat—no pulse, no blood, lifeless. At that time, I was waking up every day struggling to come up with a reason to keep living. Nobody really knew, but I was dying inside. Dying. Sad. Lost. Hopeless. Unknown. Wanting to be seen, but also wanting to run and hide. Racked with guilt and shame and regret. So, I couldn't have cared less about the academic conversation we had on stage that day. While that discussion may have stirred the neurons in the room, it never came within a mile of my busted heart. I'm not saying that what was discussed about grace wasn't accurate or factual, for it was. But it wasn't helpful. The conversation was smart but not comforting. Something was missing. The form was there, but not the substance. The facts about grace, but not the reality of grace—not the truth. And it's the truth that I was looking for that day. It's the truth we're all looking for.

Jesus did not say that religion was the truth or that his own teachings were the truth or that what people taught about him was the truth or that the Bible was the truth or the Church or any system of ethics or theological doctrine. There are individual truths in all of them, we hope and believe, but individual truths were not what Pilate was after or what you and I are after either unless I miss my guess. Truths about this or that are a dime a dozen, including religious truths. THE truth is what Pilate is after: the truth about who we are and who God is if there is a God, the truth about life, the truth about death, the truth about truth itself. That is the truth we are all of us after.

—Frederick Buechner, *The Clown in the Belfry*

A watershed moment for me? Yes. More of my life would have to be dismantled in the months and years to come. But on that day on that stage, I promised God that if given opportunities, I'd spend what was left of my life being a friend to sinners, of whom I am chief. If given the chance to preach, I'd preach one sermon—grace straight, no chaser—to one audience—the publicans and tax collectors, the screwups, misfits, liars, cheats, gypsies, tramps, and thieves.

There would be a lot more living (and dying) before I could say I'd made my peace with that shift, but that day marked me. Sue Monk Kidd describes a similar making peace moment in *The Dance of the Dissident Daughter*:

> I was driving alone early one Sunday morning in Atlanta. I stopped at a traffic light beside a small brick Baptist church. I looked at it, then at a few daffodils blooming wild in a ditch nearby . . . . Who knows what impelled me to do it—probably the need to finish and mark the forgiveness with a tangible act—but I pulled the car to the side of the road. I picked the flowers

and tied them with a string, making a little bouquet of yellow. Then I walked to the church and left the bouquet at its front doors.

We can name the places in our lives where such offerings need to be left, places where the wounds have happened, and when we are ready we can mark them with the beauty of our forgiveness. The naming and the marking release us.

Driving away from the church that day, I felt I'd made my peace.[35]

One thing we could all learn from the recovery community is that what qualifies individuals to help a group of broken-down people is to be broken down themselves. We cannot help someone in the dark if we are not keenly acquainted with the dark ourselves. You'd never, for instance, find a non-alcoholic leading an AA meeting. What qualifies a person to lead a meeting is his or her own struggle with alcohol. In the Catholic tradition, a novice priest who fails to take holy orders or is dismissed for indiscretions is referred to from that point on as a *spoiled priest*. What's interesting, though, is that in some of the old Irish Catholic stories when someone's life went off the rails, often those people would not go to the "official" Catholic priests for help or guidance or confession. No, they would seek out the spoiled priests, because those men knew what it meant to be damaged goods; they were well-acquainted with the darkness, yet they still had a shred of faith. They still believed they were beloved of God. It wasn't that they were still holding onto God, but that God was still holding onto them. A spoiled priest—that's who I was from that time on. And that God holds us—that would be my singular message.

I have learned things in the dark I could never have learned in the light,
things that have saved my life over and over again, so that there is really
only one logical conclusion: I need darkness as much as I need light.

—Barbara Brown Taylor

That was February 2016. A little over a month later, the news broke about the 2014 affair I told you about. When that news hit, my position at Willow Creek Presbyterian vanished, *poof.* As did what little public support remained for me and any hope I had of resurrecting LIBERATE. The wagons that circled included Stacie, my kids, my mother, a couple of friends, and Paul and Mary Zahl. Ironically, everyone who'd been with me on that stage just a few weeks earlier talking about grace was gone, *poof.* Like I said, there's a huge difference between grace on paper and grace in practice. Talking grace is easy—especially when everybody is behaving the way they should. "No perfect people allowed"—we love mantras like that in church mission statements and on T-shirts. But what we *truly* believe about grace is revealed in our response to someone's bad behavior, someone's failure, someone's imperfections acted out. A retired pastor friend of mine once said that he had been in the church for nearly sixty years and for nearly sixty years he has been disenchanted with the way church folk handle real sin: "Why is it that the one institution left in this world that still theoretically believes in sin, is so scandalized when they actually encounter it?" Hell, I don't know. High anthropology?

I had introduced Stacie earlier to the staff at Willow Creek, and she was warmly welcomed. But she was an eyewitness to the rapid about-face that took place when things got hotter in the kitchen. Stacie was no stranger to the ways of the religious, to the ways of ungrace. Paul Zahl once said, "The Church is almost 99.9% of the time unable to apply its greatest gift to the sinner. When it comes to grace, God's people choke." Sad and tragic, but true. Stacie had been brave enough to break her own heart by moving to Florida to be close to me. She missed her family and friends in Texas like crazy, so the Willow Creek clusterfuck was the domino that tipped the rest. She said, "I'm going back to Texas. I'm going home." I no longer had a reason to be there, and the atmosphere in Orlando was not Tullian-friendly, so I said, "Okay then, I'm going with you."

So, Stacie and I left. I drove away from all the things.

One of Stacie's relatives found us a house to rent about an hour north of Houston, in the tiny town of Willis (population 6,710), and around the first of May 2016, we moved in. Well, my possessions were there—clothes, books, etc. My body was in Texas. But my head? My heart?

TO TELL THE HOLINESS

The Apache word for myth means literally "to tell the holiness." By telling the holy, sacred stories ground a people or an individual, not merely in a landscape, but in the power that creates and preserves the land.

—Scott Russell Sanders, *Staying Put*

At first, the story I'm about to tell you will sound the polar opposite of holy, quite unholy really, if not almost unbelievable. Even as I think about it now, there's nothing about this story that makes sense in the ways we usually want stories to make sense. And while it has become hip to say, "It's not the destination, but the journey," I'm quite content to step up and say, "Well, it's both." Because while the journeys I took in the summer of 2016 were vital, the destination of those journeys was equally vital for they led to Stacie. Actually, they led me back to Stacie a couple of times. And those journeys also led me back to me, to a sense of myself that was seed-like that summer, but a seed starting to grow. This story is one full of that *sacred ambivalence*, brimming with pain and longing and sorrow and passion and humiliation, and finally love. So, the story is mythic, or holy, in my mind. And it's worth telling.

About two weeks after moving to Texas with Stacie, I fell into *The Funk*. Well, it's actually more accurate to say that I finally acted on *The Funk* that had been brewing in me for quite some time. I was happy to be with Stacie; we were having engagement and marriage talks, and there was excitement in *the new*. But I was unsettled about the pace of our relationship. Our relationship started before my divorce was final, so I had spent zero time as a single man sorting out the mess that was now my life. Everything between us had happened and was happening, so fast. My heart and head were spinning. So, the move to Texas proved too much too soon for me. I still missed all the things that had previously defined me, but instead of missing them from only a few hours away, I was now missing them from over a thousand miles away, and while that may sound like the same thing, trust me, it wasn't. Maybe someone stronger or more stable could've handled that, but I wasn't strong or stable that summer. I simply couldn't deal.

I'd already planned to go back to Florida for my daughter Genna's middle school graduation at the end of May, a long weekend where I'd join in that celebration, experience some familiarity, and then head back to Texas. What Stacie didn't know on the day I drove off, is that I wasn't sure I was coming back. Kim and I had been secretly talking, and those conversations made me realize that even though our divorce was final, we weren't over each other. I missed the woman I'd spent over half my life with and the family we'd created together. I missed having all of us under the same roof. I wanted to be back in Fort Lauderdale, my home, and with my people. With them I knew who I was. So unbeknownst to Stacie, I wasn't just headed to a middle school graduation. I was off on a mission to see if anything could be salvaged of my former life, of my former self. I said goodbye to Stacie, got in my car, and drove from Houston to south Florida. My car's odometer read over a thousand miles on that trip, but it felt like a million.

I ended up staying longer than a long weekend. I stayed almost a month. After being there a few days, I let Stacie know my plan. I told her I wasn't coming back anytime soon, that I could not move forward with our relationship if there was still a chance I could reconcile with Kim and put my family back together. At the time, Kim wanted that too. Stacie, of course, was sad and fearful, but she understood. She didn't like it, but she gave me the space to figure things out. She didn't want my heart divided any more than I did. I'd been married for twenty-one years (together for twenty-three) and that's not easy to get over. At least, it wasn't for me. Stacie understood that. And then add to the mix that all three of my kids and my first grandchild were in Fort Lauderdale; it was too much. The pull was too strong. I missed my people. Badly. And they missed me. They needed me and I needed them. We weren't the same without each other. I stayed in Kim's newly rented townhouse with her and Genna and Nate. I was back in the company of "all the things." And yet I was still confused. I'd wake one morning thinking, "this is where I belong," and the next morning I'd wake missing Stacie something crazy. In my heart, back and forth, back and forth. I was torn. Tortuously torn.

So, after about a month I decided to get in my car and drive back to Texas, back to Stacie, to try to figure out what I should do long term. I needed to see her. I thought seeing her again would help me decide what I wanted to do. She welcomed me home with open arms. She believed I was back for good. I wasn't so sure. I loved being back with her, but I was still struggling mightily on the inside. I was still really confused about where I belonged, who I was, and what I wanted. A friend of mine pulled some strings and got me a room at a convent near Houston where I could get away and be silent for three days and maybe sort out my muddled heart and head. While there, I was counseled once a day by an older and very wise nun who mostly listened to me but also reassured me that this kind of confusion, painful as it is, is not uncommon, especially in the wake of trauma. That was heartening to hear. It was a quiet and helpful three days, although when I left, I wasn't much clearer than when I arrived.

A few days after getting back from the convent, *The Funk* hit me again—same song, second verse. I was convinced that I needed to leave Texas and Stacie for good—that South Florida was where I belonged and that Kim was who I wanted to be with—needed to be with. That was the only way, I believed, I could fix what I'd broken and get my family back the way it was. Nothing mattered more to me than that. I'd only been back from Fort Lauderdale for about two weeks when Stacie came home from work one evening and I said, "I gotta go. But this time I'm not coming back. I'm going to stay."

See how unholy this sounds? It sounds like the diary of a madman, a crazed lunatic collecting his jar of hearts while he himself didn't know his ass from a hole in the ground. If Stacie's reaction to my first *Funk* was sadness and fear, the second *Funk* elicited a hell-hath-no-fury response. She said, "Then leave now!"

And I did. I packed all my stuff, got in my car, and drove once again to Fort Lauderdale convinced in my lizard brain that I could indeed do what all the king's horses and all the king's men couldn't—put my Humpty Dumpty world back together again.

TRUST GOD WITH THIS

I didn't stay in Kim's townhouse the second time around. I stayed at a friend's house. Kim was also put off by my flip-floppiness and lack of transparency. But I went as far as buying her an engagement ring and planning a proposal such was my confused resolve to fix it all. This time I was in Fort Lauderdale for about six weeks, which I guess was sufficient time for me to realize that life there had moved on without me. They didn't need a nurse or a hero. They could've used someone who knew who he was, and what he really wanted.

> All romantic love is conditional in that the condition is a person's essential nature. Their them-ness. If your love for a person isn't predicated on the condition that they are them right now as they are, and in instead predicated on their need for that love, or on your thinking that you could do a good job of making that person happier or "better," then you are a nurse . . . . But you are not a lover. You are not in love . . . to enjoy being the hero who swoops in and saves the day is to have a deep desire for self-annihilation. Saving someone feels easy, compared to asking yourself who the hell you are and what you want and how you want to be loved and by whom. Compared to asking, How might I care for myself?
>
> —C J Hauser, *The Crane Wife*

My old life, the one I gave it one more try to save? Over, over and done. My possible new life, the one with Stacie in Texas? It sure felt over, a bridge I'd torched. I didn't have anywhere to go so, homeless and hopeless, I got in my car (my car and I became really close that summer) and drove to my mom's in North Carolina. A mother's love is not a slight thing, I'm here to tell you, and she welcomed me in. Meanwhile, back in Texas, Stacie had been in agonizing conversations almost daily with Mary Zahl about me and my unhinged journeys. Stacie had wondered if she should do something, say something, break our silence. Mary told Stacie: "Trust God with this. Just be still. If Tullian comes back, you want it to be because God brought him back."

It took about a week to get from Fort Lauderdale to my mom's because I stopped a few times along the way to visit and stay with friends. During that week, I broke the silence between Stacie and me. We talked on the phone a couple times and exchanged a few emails and texts. Those conversations were uncomfortable, hard, and short-lived. But about two weeks after I arrived at my mom's, I broke the silence again. I sent Stacie a picture of a sunrise (I'd been up all night chain-smoking cigarettes) and confessed. I apologized for my behavior, tried my best to describe (not necessarily explain) what had happened. I also told her what I realized I wanted, better yet *who*—her. She knew me and loved me enough to know that my struggle had been distressingly real, that I had been genuinely confused for understandable reasons. So, was I hopeful she would give me another chance? Absolutely. Did I think she would? I wasn't sure. Resilient and forgiving as she is, I had hurt her; I'd not been careful with her heart. So, I had some serious doubts.

Sometimes telling the holiness doesn't end with much happiness. Sometimes the wounds are too great, and the break is too wide. And yet sometimes it's as if the story itself resists that sadness, not with a bright red bow, but with a hushed, "I forgive you, Tullian. Come back." So, my buddy (my car) and I drove from North Carolina to just outside Houston, back to the small Texas town of Willis (population 6,710), to the rented house where Stacie lived. That was late July 2016. We got engaged, and Stacie and I were married a month later in a small ceremony surrounded by family and friends.

Was it God who brought me back to Stacie after the summer of *Funks*? You can answer a question like that quickly when love is young and "full of flowers and heart-shaped boxes." But Stacie and I met on the other side of failure and loss, and we tend to sit with questions like that a little longer. As of this writing, we've sat with that question for seven years, seven married years, and when we pause and tell the holiness, our answer is, "Yes. God did."

> To live in this world
> you must be able
> to do three things:
> to love what is mortal;
> to hold it
> against your bones knowing
> your own life depends on it;
> and, when the time comes to let it go,
> to let it go.
>
> —Mary Oliver, "In Blackwater Woods"

Part 3

THE MENDED HEART

Chapter 7
HOME BY ANOTHER WAY

In 2017, twenty-three-year-old Australian Ricky Garard made his first appearance at the CrossFit Games. Relatively unknown in the world of competitive fitness, Garard ended the games in third place overall, with a spot on the podium and a place in the hearts of fans. Then, in a sudden whirlwind of events, Garard was stripped of his medal and his spot on the podium. He'd tested positive for PEDs—performance-enhancing drugs. He admitted to taking them knowingly, and the shorter version of a longer story concluded with Ricky Garard being handed a four-year suspension and a scarlet letter of sorts (a *cheater*) in the sport.

The CrossFit Games do not exist on the level of, say, the Olympics or the National Football League. The coverage is much smaller, in a way almost a niche. That's changing, gradually, but unless you follow that world and its athletes closely, you may not have any context for that incident or have any earthly idea who or what a Ricky Garard is. Fans were divided in their support; some felt the suspension too harsh, some not harsh enough, and a few felt it just right.

But the 2022 CrossFit Games saw the return of Ricky Garard. After the dust had settled on a weekend of grueling fitness challenges, Garard was back on the podium in the bronze spot he was stripped of in 2017, this time "clean," this time having prevailed, as some said, "fair and square." In 2022, Ricky Garard was the third fittest man on earth. In an interview, he described the competition floor as "a place where I belong, a place I was born to be, a place that I thrive, a place that I can achieve my dreams, a place that has shaped who I am since the age of 5, a place where I have succeeded, failed and learnt my biggest lessons, a place I think about every day."[36]

You could say Ricky Garard was describing coming *home*.

I'm no Ricky Garard, although I am a bit of a fitness freak. But I was banned for being far too comfortable with what could metaphorically be called drugs that enhanced a performance-riddled celebrity brain. I took them knowingly and got caught. And I've had quite the journey coming back, coming home.

The world of high-profile churches and their pastors is somewhat like the CrossFit world. It gets coverage, especially (and often only) when there's scandal, but it's often only a blip then the news cycle moves on. If you're in that world, it can seem like everything. But if you're not, it's not.

When I resigned from Coral Ridge Presbyterian Church in 2015 and was subsequently stripped of my professional credentials, it felt like that was everything everybody was talking about. I'm not saying it wasn't news, because it was. All the major national media outlets reported on it, and in the religious world it was *the* news story that summer and fall. But think back to 2015—Charlie Hebdo attack in Paris, the deaths of Walter Scott and Freddie Gray at the hands of police officers, a prison break in New York, the Charleston Church and other mass shootings, the Pope's visit to the US, and the list goes on. As usual, there was a lot going on in the larger world. So, while it may have seemed like all eyes were on me and my personal collapse, they weren't. In the grand scheme of things in 2015, my sordid story was a blip on the radar.

And it was even less than a blip on God's.

To say that might seem dismissive, like I'm minimizing my sin or suggesting that God didn't care about me or what I had done. But that's not what I mean. What I mean is that the sins we can't forget, God doesn't even remember. That's right. He doesn't even remember. It's not that he *can't* remember. It's better than that—he *chooses* to not remember. "For I will forgive their wickedness and remember their sins no more" Hebrews 8:12 NIV.

According to Robert Capon, this means that "Jesus takes all of our badness down into the forgettery of his death and offers to the Father only what is held in the memory of his resurrection." [37] So, while I have to live the rest of my life with the consequences of my choices during that season—the most painful being watching those I love suffer the lifelong effects of decisions I made— I never have to deal with God being against me because of my screwups. Ever.

So, less than a blip.

God is a God of grace and mercy, not karma. And that means, among other things, that God doesn't dole out misery in proportion to our sin. Pain is not God's payback for bad behavior. "He does not deal with us according to our sins, nor repay us according to our iniquities" (Psalm 103:10 ESV). Now, let me be very clear, we do experience the consequences of our actions. Destructive decisions have destructive results. Trust me, I know. But that is a very different thing than concluding that the anguish we experience because of horrible decisions we've made is God "getting us back" for what we've done or failed to do. That would make God a caricature of the "just-wait-till-your-father-gets-home" father who enjoys trotting us out to the woodshed when we screw up. That's not who God is. I know this to be true. But I've also found it really hard to believe that God is for me, and not against me, when everything around me seems to prove otherwise. That feeling sends me into pissed-off overdrive.

I remember being so angry with God when my life fell apart. I mean, at first, I braced myself and *took it like a man* because I knew I'd screwed up and had to pay the price. Fair enough, more than fair enough. But, as the fallout and public rancor seemed to drag on and on and on with no end in sight, it started to feel unfair, like God was getting me back. Hell, I knew lots of people who'd done far worse stuff than me, so it seemed, and they were suffering far less than me, so it seemed. I had it out with God a lot during that time. The times I could pray (which weren't very often), I couldn't do it without cussing and screaming. I'd read the anguished cries of the psalmist, preached them even, but they had rarely been a part of my prayer life up to that point. But there I was, giving God the big swollen middle finger (and that's no metaphor).

Want to hear more? Okay, sure. I remember one time in particular when things seemed to be leveling out a bit. A little time had passed; it had been a couple years, and much of the public and private vitriol had eased, and some new doors were beginning to open. My thinking was *Thank God*. One opportunity in particular had a lot of promise. I was approached by a publisher that was keenly interested in publishing a revised version of one of my books. I was excited. They were excited. I was offered, and I signed, a contract. Maybe the clouds were breaking, maybe the sun might shine again.

Stacie and I were visiting my mom in North Carolina and went with her one night to my grandad's conference center, The Cove, to hear a speaker my mom wanted to hear. Right before we walked in, I got an email notification. I opened it to find a brief deflating message from the publisher letting me know that they would not be publishing the book; the contract I'd signed was rescinded, game over—and only weeks before the scheduled release date. The reason? Fear of public blowback for publishing a "canceled" Christian. Concise and gutting, not to mention illegal. I bolted to the only space that held some privacy—the men's room—and lost my shit. I returned red-faced and teary-eyed to Stacie and my mom; we found our seats and sat down to the opening worship song for the evening—"Good, Good Father"—and I thought, "Nope, no way. That's bullshit. I'm not singing this crap." By the looks on their angelic faces, everyone around me seemed to be lost in lovey-dovey thoughts of a good, good God while I wanted to burn the goddamn house down. Whatever doesn't kill you makes you stronger? Well, maybe, unless it kills you, and that night took me out.

Author Charlie Shedd recounts a note his wife left on the kitchen counter one morning after they fought the night before:

Dear Charlie, I hate you.
Love, Martha

That night my post-it psalm to God would've been:

Dear God, I hate you.
Love, Tullian

There will be nights or days when you can't sing "Good, Good Father." It simply doesn't truck with your current reality. I'd caution you away from the "just keep singing anyway, fake it till you make it" attitude.

I'd say go to your equivalent of "the men's room" and lose your shit. God is fully capable of handling my anguish, yours too. And that's good, good news. Yes, the good news for recidivist screwups like me (and you) is that God does not relate to us on the basis of what we do or don't do, even what we pray or can't. The way God feels about us is in no way affected by the way we feel about him. He relates to us on the basis of grace—the seemingly chaotic, cavalier nature of his too-good-to-be-true, one-way love. Grace means there is nothing I can do to make God love me more, and nothing I can do to make God love me less. Grace is recklessly generous, uncomfortably promiscuous. It doesn't use sticks or carrots. It doesn't keep score. As Robert Capon puts it, "Grace works without requiring anything on our part. It's not expensive. It's not even cheap. It's free."[38] It refuses to be controlled by our innate sense of fairness, reciprocity, and evenhandedness. It defies logic. It has nothing to do with earning, merit, or deservedness. It's opposed to what's owed. It's a liberating contradiction between what we deserve and what we get. Grace is unconditional acceptance given to an undeserving person by an unobligated giver. In Frederick Buechner's memorable book *Wishful Thinking*, he describes grace this way as he talks about the apostle Paul hearing God's voice on the road to Damascus:

> Paul also discovered that all the Brownie points he had been trying to rack up as a super-Pharisee had been pointless. God did business with you not because of who you were but because of who he was . . . . At a moment in his life when he had the least reason to expect it, Paul was staggered by the idea that no matter who you are or what you've done, God wants you on his side. There is nothing you have to do or be. It's on the house. It goes with the territory. God has "justified you," lined you up . . . ."[39]

That's grace. It's on the house. Your pardon is full and final. No strings attached. No ifs, ands, or buts. No conditions. No paybacks. No boomerangs. Before God you are loved and clean . . . even when you're losing your shit.

COWBOYS AND ANGELS

In the fall of 2016, my new wife, Stacie, and I were living in Willis, Texas. The first year of marriage for any couple has its challenges, but if one of you is (no lie) going through a version of soul detox/rehab, it's . . . I don't even know what to call it . . . I'll just say *hard*. Stacie was working for a title company, and I was at home doing the dishes, folding clothes, going to the gym every day, and going to counseling twice a week trying to figure out not only what the hell happened to my life, but what the hell was I supposed to do with the rest of it, and most importantly, who the hell I was. That's when the cowboy called.

> Surely the Lord is in this place, and I did not know it.
>
> —Genesis 28:16 ESV

That verse is Jacob talking, after he wakes from his dream of the stairway to heaven, after he's deceived his father, and after he's cheated his brother. He'd been up to a lot of no good, yet he rouses awake with an awareness of the nearness of God. I'd say let's not chalk that up to Jacob's capacity for awareness but rather God's commitment to nearness. I didn't have an angel dream like Jacob, but my phone rang in January 2017, and it was Mark Grimes who I surely didn't think was an angel at first, but I came to believe differently.

Mark pastors the Caney Creek Cowboy Church in Grangerland, Texas. If you know about cowboy church culture, then you know.

If you don't, they're local gatherings often in a barn or arena setting where the vibe is come-as-you-are, the preaching is straightforwardly plain, the priestly vestments are boots, buckles, and blue jeans; when it comes to music there's often a fiddle in the band, and you're welcome to hitch your horse outside. Seriously, that's not an exaggeration. The tagline of Caney Creek Cowboy Church is "Boots or Suits, Horses or Harleys, Everyone is Welcome."

Mark had heard I was in the area, and he knew my story from the news cycles. He got my number from Stacie's dad who plays electric guitar in the church band. When Mark called, he told me he was interested in writing a book and asked if I'd be willing to meet him for lunch to advise him on the book writing and publishing process. I had nothing but time on my hands, so I agreed. Even though I had no idea what Mark looked like, when he showed up, I knew it was him. Big truck, big hat, big buckle, big boots, big boy. As different as we were, we hit it off immediately. We talked about the book he wanted to write for a few minutes, but then he abruptly and spontaneously changed the subject. He looked at me and put his cards on the table, "How would you like to come work with me at the church? Given your experience, you could really help me develop some things, and it'd give you some more time to heal a little." I wasn't quite sure I heard him right, so I asked him to repeat the offer. He did, and I'd heard him right the first time. About the time I want to go ballistic on the church culture of our day for being a bunch of Chicken-Littles in khakis and blue blazers, I remember moments like that, moments when the church steps up and does what the church was born to do, and I back off and calm down (for a little while).

When Stacie came home from work that day, I told her about my lunch and Mark's offer. She was a little scared; I was a little scared. There's a scene in that classic Christmas movie *It's a Wonderful Life* where a young George Bailey has been instructed to deliver what he knows to be, due to a mix-up, a deadly prescription. As he pauses, wondering what to do, there's a cigarette ad sign on the drugstore wall behind him that reads: "Ask Dad, he knows." The boy-George then takes off for his father's loan office to withdraw some wisdom. I needed some Dad-wisdom like that, and since my amazingly gracious and supernaturally wise dad died back in 2010, I called my friend and father-figure Paul Zahl to see what he thought I should do. Paul knows me, and I mean knows me. He knows I'm South Florida, like *Miami Vice* vibes, about as far as you can get from Wranglers and belt buckles that double as satellite dishes. I trust him implicitly. So, after Stacie and I thoroughly explained the situation and answered all of Paul's clarification questions as best we could, Paul surprisingly said, "Tullian, I think it's perfect for you. It's the next stop on the road home."

So, a few days later, Stacie and I met with Mark, thanked him for the invitation, and put two conditions on the table. First, nobody could know I was there; in other words, the church couldn't "use me to attract people," that kind of thing. Second, it would have to be an independent contractor relationship, not a staff position. I told him I would be happy to help the church in a behind-the-scenes kind of way, but for some necessary healing to take place, I needed to be off anyone's radar. I needed to serve with no recognition and no fanfare. I needed distance and silence from where I'd been.

What does the son do? He turns away, loses courage, goes outdoors to feed with wild things, lives among dens and hunts, eats distance and silence . . .

—Robert Bly, "Fifty Males Sitting Together"

Mark agreed. I wrote up a six-month contract, and it was one of the most healing experiences I've ever had. Let me attempt to explain.

The people with whom I spent the next six months? Not my demographic, not my people. By that I mean not the kind of people I was used to being around. These were hard-working, blue-collar country people, most of whose stories of heartbreak and ruin made mine look small in comparison. In the broader church world, my sin had been elevated to the point of being almost unforgivable. The shame and guilt associated with what I'd done was overwhelmingly big. And then suddenly I was thrust into an unfamiliar world where the community was very well acquainted with grief: prison, divorces, addictions, adulteries, overdoses, legal issues like you wouldn't believe (or maybe you would). This church was literally a country song. It wasn't that those realities weren't present where I'd come from; they were, but they weren't held in common so to speak, cards out on the table. You could say at Caney Creek sin abounded. Yes, that means grace abounded more, but let me tell you sin abounded a lot. Those large-hearted, beautifully busted-up people learned of what I'd done and essentially said, "Welcome. You're one of us." They never blinked, not once. Grace was there, on the house.

Wait. I can't say everyone felt that way about me. I remember one woman in particular who knew who I was and what I'd done, or at least what people had said I'd done. She went to Mark and expressed her concerns—sort of a "Pastor, what are you doing here?" Mark told her that he and about 85% of the people in the congregation had done as much and worse, and the truth was they had. He told her, "This is the right thing to do." After about three months of me being there and getting to know the people and them getting to know me, this woman came to me in tears after a service. She told me what she'd said to Mark when I first arrived, and then she said, "Tullian, I'm so sorry. I judged you without knowing you. I'm sorry." Now that may sound like a Touched-By-An-Angel-moment or something, but it wasn't. The clouds didn't lift; no orchestra began playing in the background. It was simply grace working its way deeper into her life and deeper into mine, and both of us being the better for it going forward. The people there weren't angels. They were better than that. They were fallen flesh and blood who'd experienced grace, and they wanted to pass it on, to get back to something foundational, something called love.

There's a question in Ken Burns's 2019 documentary *Country Music*, a question repeatedly asked: "Who are we?" What unfolds is an eye and ear opening look at not only who Americans are, but also who humans are. Burns covers well-known figures like Johnny Cash and George Jones and Dolly Parton, noting not just their successes, but their failures too, maybe those failures even more, their sins of commission and omission. As *Commonweal* editor Matthew Sitman wrote about Burns' work: "Country Music tells story after story like this—and it is these stories, and the songs of those who lived them, that provide another way of answering Burns's question. Who are we? We are addicts and drunks. We are poor and hungry. We break our promises and live with regret over the pain we cause others. We are selfish, we are sinners, we hope one day to be saints. We are frail creatures who know we are destined to die. We try, again and again, to "get back to the basics of love."

—"E Pluribus Country," *Dissent Magazine*, Winter 2020

Those words describe for me the grace-filled country people of Caney Creek Cowboy Church. For the question—"who are we?"—they knew the answer, because they all had failure stories; they'd lived them and were still living them—stories shot through with frailty but buoyed by grace and redemption, again and again. They'd learned the notes. They sang the strains of the beloved and invited me to sing along.

A MONTH OF SUNDAYS

I tell the Caney Creek story not primarily because it has a fallen pastor in it, but because it has a broken human in it, a human who fell and crashed and burned and screwed it all up. The moment we think there's some difference between fallen "people" and fallen "pastors," it's quite clear we've lost the thread. Now, do I believe there's something in that story of value for pastors who've fallen and churches whose pastors have fallen and denominations who have churches with pastors who've fallen? I absolutely do. We toss the word *healing* around quite easily these days; sometimes I'm not even sure what we're talking about. But if healing, in the sense of mending a broken bone so the arm or leg can function again, is what is wanted and needed, then in the wake of those horrible experiences, somehow that pastor needs to "eat distance and silence" as Bly said. He or she needs to go to an *anti-Cheers*—where nobody knows your name. A place where nobody cares about who your grandfather was, or is impressed that you've written books and once pastored a megachurch, or anything like that. Pastors need a safe place to land and a soft place to fall, not cushy but soft. Fallen people ought to be able to fall, when they inevitably do (again and again), into the hands of a loving people.

If you find yourself in the company of people whose hearts have been captured by grace, count yourself lucky. They love us despite our messy lives, stay connected to us through our struggles, always holding out the hope of redemption. You don't see hard edges, dogmatism, or self-righteous judgment from gracious people. There's a tenderness about them that opens doors that had been previously bolted shut. People who have been transformed by grace have a special place in their hearts for those living in the shadows of society. They're easily moved by stories of suffering and step into the breach to heal.

—Peter Wehner

One of John Updike's novels is titled *A Month of Sundays*. It tells the story of Reverend Tom Marshfield who, in the wake of sexual scandal, is sent west from his Midwestern parish to a desert retreat center dedicated to rest, recreation, and spiritual renewal. Just so you know, when it comes to sexual sin, Marshfield is a repeat offender. As a part of his "healing," he is required to use the morning hours to keep a journal, to essentially write sermons that function as a sort of therapy. Those thirty-one entries are the building blocks for Updike's story. The rest of Marshfield's time is free—he can play golf or drink or lounge by the pool or whatever he wants to do at the rather upscale retreat center populated by other dysfunctional White Protestant American clergymen; in other words, men just like him.[40]

Now when it comes to books by John Updike, *A Month of Sundays* is not his best—far from it, most would agree. But it is interesting that in this story, the reverend doesn't heal, even in such an Edenic atmosphere where one might believe it would be impossible not to. Oh, he may have left rested, having caught up on some needed sleep, and also possibly emerged with a nice tan, but healed? Nope.

Even with the required journal work, Marshfield never grew beyond the isolation and defensiveness of his ego, that ego being the thing that got him in all his trouble in the first place.

My point is this. I don't have all the answers for what to do when a pastor crashes and burns. I know there are some rather elaborate processes available. All I have is my story and what I experienced. And in light of that, I believe that a fallen leader's healing needs to involve some variation on a theme of *retreat*—not the desert center retreat variety but more the Caney Creek Cowboy Church reality. And furthermore, that retreat should be not merely to a place but also to a people, a people not like the fallen leader. In that place and with those people, that leader can "eat distance and silence" and be uncomfortable and awkward and blunder around and try to find some footing, but hopefully most of all find grace. For grace, in company, is what mends.

Healing is impossible in loneliness; it is the opposite of loneliness. Conviviality is healing. To be healed we must come with all the other creatures to the feast of Creation.

—Wendell Berry

GRACE FOR THE DISGRACED

If I had a dollar for every Christian leader (including me) exposed for their sin and deposed from their positions in the last few years, I'd have a stack of dollars. Allegations (and in some cases, admissions) of adultery, addiction, and various forms of abuse have left lives, hearts, marriages, and churches in rubble. Each case has its own distinctives, but all of them are violent "unravelings" of a world that *used to be*.

It would be foolish to attempt to speak to the incidents themselves because I don't have all the facts. And I definitely don't believe everything I read online (please tell me you don't either). In some severe cases, illegal offenses such as sexual, physical, or financial crimes have taken place. When that's the case, it's time for the state to step in, prosecute, and punish. At the same time, I also believe that these things happen inside a complex framework of falleness that only God can fully know and understand, and that in all these situations, real people are involved—children, families, friends, churches.

These real people include the leaders themselves—both men and women. Their struggle with the aftershocks of their sin usually gets relegated to the back of the line. But I believe they deserve better. The ones that dominate media coverage are so-called "celebrity pastors," but most are largely unknown outside their communities. Famous or not, however, when they have been exposed, most live isolated and ashamed inside the consequences of their own damn fault.

I know this all too well. I've bled from those same self-induced injuries. I guess because my story is fairly well-known, many of these former ministers have reached out to me. And now, on their behalf, I reach out to the church. The words and thoughts that follow from here to the end of this chapter were a collaborative effort between my good friend Chad Bird and me.

Every individual act of sin has communal repercussions. There's no vacuum. This is why when one person sins, every person around them suffers—including the one that sinned. Of course, everyone experiences a different dimension of suffering. The ones sinned against experience the suffering of betrayal and injustice, hurt and confusion—just to name a few. The one who sinned experiences the suffering of guilt and shame and regret and, oftentimes, ostracism. Both experience loss at various levels.

But here is the uncomfortable kicker: the grace of God is for both parties. The good news of God's unconditional love and outrageous mercy has always and forever been for sufferers, regardless of whether the suffering is self-induced or caused by someone else. If the good news of God's forgiving and restorative grace isn't for everybody, then it isn't for anybody.

We are told in James 1:19 that "everyone should be quick to listen, slow to speak and slow to become angry" (NRSV). But when a Christian leader takes a dive, that verse suddenly becomes extra-canonical or something. People comment, people gossip, people speculate, people report, people talk, people tweet, people blog. But people also watch. How will a group of forgiven sinners handle a fellow sinner who needs forgiveness? Is the Christian community a safe or scary place to bottom out? These are not rhetorical questions. They're real.

HOW WILL THE CHRISTIAN COMMUNITY REACT?

To be clear, I'm *not* talking about a Christian leader being restored to his or her position of leadership. In each of the cases that I'm aware of, these leaders have needed to step down and step away from leadership in the church—maybe for a time, and maybe forever. In each case I'm aware of, including mine, something was amiss personally and privately long before everything blew up publicly. There needs to be grieving and repentance and wrestling on a personal as well as communal level, and that takes time. A long time.

I'm also not talking about being soft on sin, sweeping the bad behavior under the rug, or minimizing the consequences. Sin is not theoretical. It happens in real time with real people and real consequences that must be really dealt with. No condemnation (Romans 8:1) does *not* mean no consequences. But what's equally important is that the inescapable reality of consequences does *not* mean the presence of condemnation.

If God is who we say God is, then real sin can only be met with real forgiveness. In fact, if what we know about grace has any bearing on our lives, then redemption—not retribution—ought to be our deepest longing. It is the only thing that has a shot of making any difference or bringing about genuine healing for everybody. The cross shows us that God is serious about sin, and we should therefore take sin seriously. But (and this is the part that often seems missing when scandal in church leadership happens), the cross also shows us that God is serious about redemption, restoration, and forgiving sins, and we should take *that* seriously too.

THREE DAYS AWAY FROM A TABLOID HEADLINE

The grace of God is not reserved for the "well-behaved." Full stop. Yet that is exactly the message we send every time the word *fall* is used in reference to someone who is by nature already fallen. These ministers (people) are sinners, just like everybody they ever led. That in no way justifies destructive behavior, diminishes the sting of consequences, or minimizes the harming effects of destructive choices. But c'mon, theoretical grace is good for nothing. If we're only okay with preaching grace in theory, but not when someone—even an esteemed leader—is in need of it, then we should close up shop.

Sadness, grief, and prayer are understandable responses to a scandal in the pastorate, but complete surprise or total shock is another matter. Shock is telling, for it reveals that somewhere along the way, we've come to believe that there is a fundamental difference between church leaders and church goers—that somehow leaders are less sinful. Yes, there are *functional* differences between church leaders and church goers, but not *fundamental* differences. The idea that congregants and clergy don't struggle with the same things is hands down dangerous. Pastors are human beings with all the same flaws, fears, and sinful tendencies that the rest of humanity has. They don't live outside the bounds of reality or human nature. My friend Jacob Smith once said that all of us are three bad days away from becoming a tabloid headline, and most of us are already on day two. But you might ask, what about "to whom much is given?" From where I stand now, I'd say, "much must also be forgiven." If the stakes are higher, why not the mercy?

It is anti-Christian to remember people primarily by the scandalous things they've done. We love to whittle an entire life story down to a single scene. Then, with the authority invested in us by the state of self-righteousness, we proclaim, "This, and nothing else, is who you are." But the truth is, all of us (including disgraced Christian leaders) are more complicated than the singular narrative by which most people identify us. We have done some very good things. And we have done some very bad things. And many days we stir a mean cocktail of both. Sadly, most people remember only the bad. Thankfully, we have a God who remembers only the good. If we want to reduce our life story down to one adjective, if we want to whittle our biography down to a single word, then let's take a cue from Christ when he calls us *Beloved*.

How can the church make it clear to clergy, trapped inside the shame-filled prison of their sins, that they too are Beloved?

One could hardly imagine a greater discrepancy between the typical response to "fallen" Christian leaders and what we saw in that Charleston, South Carolina, courthouse in 2015. The world stood slack-jawed as members of the Emanuel AME church lined up to speak forgiveness to the white man who murdered nine of their fellow black church members in cold blood. And not just lip service forgiveness either. As Nadine Collier, daughter of Ethel Lance who was gunned down, said, "You hurt me, you have hurt a lot of people. But I forgive you." You'll notice that these ladies didn't wait for a display of repentance or sorrow to issue their statement. Grace came first. In the eloquence of my friend David Zahl: "Unconditional love doesn't wait for the correct response; it produces it."

Unconditional love is purposefully blind. It's blind to whether its recipient stood in the pulpit or sat in the pew. It's blind to whether the sin hurt many or only a few. It's blind to the fake hierarchy of big sins and little sins that is the working assumption in most religious circles. Unconditional love is blind to everything but the ones who stand there—or lie there—broken, shamed, guilty, and dying to hear even a single voice that says, "I love you. I forgive you."

That love is like the voice of God at the beginning of Genesis: it's creative. For the ones who reside in the darkness of guilt, it says, "Let there be the light of hope for them." For those who are dying to taste even a drop of mercy, it says, "Let the waters of absolution flow into that parched heart." Unconditional love comes to that person whose life has been uncreated, and it speaks creative words of life once more. And God sees that it is good. He sees that it is very good.

SOLIDARITY WITH THE "UNCLEAN"

The greatest gift the church can give to former ministers is to treat them, not as those who once preached in front of a congregation, but as those who stand with them now at the foot of the cross. The preachers become those preached to—by the very ones to whom they ministered. Sheep become shepherds to the former shepherd. This is admittedly a challenge, but a challenge that rests at the heart of grace itself. In other words, it's crazy damn hard. But grace knows no gradations of sin, no categories of clergy and lay, no scales of fat and skinny wrongs. As in the parable that Jesus told in Matthew 20, everyone gets paid the same, whether they worked in the vineyard all day or only an hour, whether they harvested two grapes or two thousand, whether they led a work crew or took a smoke break every twenty minutes. The owner of the vineyard, *out of his mercy,* writes everyone the same paycheck. It's the paycheck of unearned, undeserved love for all in the vineyard, no matter who they are or what they've done. In that way, grace is karma's worst nightmare: we get the very opposite of what we deserve.

If the church truly wants to stand apart from the world, it will consistently stand alongside those who have been disgraced, and that includes ministers. It will risk being falsely attacked as "soft on sin" because it knows how hard life is when guilt and shame are one's only companions. Rather than shooting the wounded, it will pick them up and carry them to safety, to rehab, to repentance, to whatever it takes for deep healing to happen. While the world drinks itself drunk on outrage of every kind, the church will exercise outrageous grace and scandalous mercy that doggedly refuses to give up on those ensnared by destructiveness.

When a leper approached Jesus to ask for healing, he did an astonishing thing. Before Jesus spoke, before anything else, "he stretched out his hand and touched him" (Matthew 8:3 ESV). Jesus touched the untouchable. Solidarity with the unclean preceded everything else. We are to do likewise; that's the church's calling. Before we preach, before we teach, before we do anything else, we stretch out our hands and touch the sinner. It's putting some skin in mercy's game, getting out of the stands, and onto the field. By doing so, we open up incredible opportunities for healing, not only for the one wounded, but also for the community as a whole. A church that is built on the reality of grace and forgiveness for everyone (even the most disgraced Christian), is also a community that experiences its own healing when it embraces rather than ostracizes fallen leaders. The medicine of mercy works both ways, for the giver and the receiver. It heals individuals and the community. The church, in forgiving others, experiences the power of that forgiveness in its own life.

THE RARE MERCY OF UNCONDITIONAL LOVE

How beautiful to be right on the Father's heels as he runs out to welcome the prodigals. That gives a fuller meaning to *"how beautiful on the mountains are the feet of those . . ."*, huh? And that means there will be tears of joy too, and big bear-hugs followed by a feast for all, and laughter, man oh man, the hilarity of grace ringing throughout the valley . . . for the one who was dead is alive again. The one who was lost is found. The one who wandered is home.

But yes, in light of all that poetic partying, the logical follow-up question to all this would be: But how long does the mending take? What length of time qualifies as true restoration? Six weeks? Six months? Two years? Ten years? I don't know, and I feel like anyone saying there's a standard timeframe to follow is naive. As sin is always specific, so is grace or healing or restoration—it's always specific to the person. I was graced with six months at Caney Creek, and then another handful at a place, interestingly enough, called Living Faith (for it was). I'll come back to the question of "how long?" in the next chapter.

Chapter 8
LIVING FAITH

Did I love Mark Grimes and the people of Caney Creek Cowboy Church? Absolutely. In fact, I still do. Mark and I stay in touch to this day. But because more than one thing can be true at the same time, I was also itchin' to get back to southeast Florida. Because southeast Florida was home; it was me. Beaches and balmy weather, palm trees and ocean breezes, sunburns and saltwater, city nights and rooftops. All of it. The symphony of lights, sights, and sounds that infuse the ethos of southeast Florida is magical to me. It loosens me up, chills me out, and makes me dreamy. Southeast Florida is the language of my soul. Southeast Florida is poetry.

> Poetry, at its best, is the language your soul would speak if you could teach your soul to speak.
>
> —Jim Harrison

In the spring of 2017, I received a Facebook message from my friend Pat Thurmer. Pat pastored Living Faith Lutheran Church

in Cape Coral, Florida, which is on the southwest coast of Florida.
We'd met when Pat would bring a group from his church over to the
LIBERATE conference that I hosted every year in Fort Lauderdale.
His message to me in 2017 felt curious; he wondered how I was doing,
what I was up to. So we set up a time to talk, and on our call I told
him I was living in Texas with my new wife. I told him what I'd been
doing at Caney Creek, but I also confessed that I really didn't know
what was next and that was causing me to feel lost.

Pat said:

> Let me be the first to tell you our church loves you.
> We believe that your best days are ahead of you. And,
> while I can't offer you a job because we are a small church
> with an even smaller budget, if you and Stacie were to
> ever move here, what I can offer you is a community of
> people—a church—committed to your continued care
> and restoration.

It's not every day you have a conversation like that, a conversation
overflowing with a living faith. Stacie and I talked about Pat's call,
and several weeks later, the church flew us out there (on their
dime) to check things out, sort of a scouting expedition for us and
them. We thoroughly enjoyed the time and the people, then flew
back to Texas.

The difference between the southwest coast of Florida, where
Living Faith is, and the southeast coast of Florida, where I'm from,
is pretty massive in every way. The weather is the same, for the
most part, but everything else is different—the culture, the pace,
the people, the landscape. I had never been to Cape Coral before
that trip. It was foreign territory to me. And neither Stacie nor I
were particularly attracted to the area itself. But it would put me

only two hours from Fort Lauderdale, where all my familiar was, and that got me excited. Now Stacie's from Texas. That's where all her family lives—parents, siblings, kids, cousins, dogs, cows, everybody. No one in her large, extended family lives outside of Texas. No one. So again, as multiple things can be true at the same time, while Stacie knew I longed for Florida, she was also in heaven being back in Texas around all her family. And I could see that—the joy in her face was unmistakable.

We wrestled with what to do. We sought counsel from trusted friends and family members. We were trying to hear God, see God, and feel God; while we both were blessed immeasurably by Caney Creek, we both also sensed that season was coming to a close. As we wrestled, I connected Pat Thurmer with Paul Zahl, and told Pat, "Look, Paul knows my story, all of it, and I want the cards on the table, so talk to him, ask questions, whatever you want. And if you decide there's too much carnage, I'll understand." After a few weeks, Living Faith invited us to visit again (on their dime). Stacie and I flew there, and on that second visit, we both felt that was the next step for us. We couldn't see anything beyond that, no destination or completed picture, but it was the next step, or the next two or three in front of us. And that was enough. I've learned that's always enough.

> E. L. Doctorow once said that "Writing a novel is like driving a car at night. You can see only as far as your headlights, but you can make the whole trip that way." You don't have to see where you're going, you don't have to see your destination or everything you will pass along the way. You just have to see two or three feet ahead of you. This is right up there with the best advice on writing, or life, I have ever heard.[41]
>
> —Anne Lamott, *Bird by Bird*

In John 1:14, Jesus is described as full of "grace and truth."

> And the Word became flesh and dwelt among us,
> and we have seen his glory, glory as of the only Son from
> the Father, full of grace and truth (ESV).

Grace and truth. They're not so much two sides of the same coin as twin streams that travel together, always. They are, after all, "the Word," not "the words." The grace of truth and the truth of grace. And in different ways, because churches, like people, have personalities, Caney Creek and Living Faith both offered me their own flavors of God's graceful truth and truthful grace. I can see now I needed Caney Creek's first. If they'd been switched in order, I would have missed something, something vital to what, I believe, God was trying to do. If I'd been in charge, I would've chosen Living Faith/Florida first. But if there's anything I've learned on this road, it's that I'm not in charge. Thank God. So, back to Florida was the next phase of my rehab. And kinda like going on a bear hunt and encountering wavy grass and mushroom patches and wide rivers, I couldn't go around it or under it or over it; I had to go through it. But I won't lie. Even though it wasn't the southeast coast of Florida where I'm from, the fact that it was in Florida at all? Huge for me. Huge!

SCREW IT, I'LL GO FIRST

Stacie and I moved to Fort Myers (a neighboring city to Cape Coral) in September 2017. A few months prior to that, I'd had a strong sense that God wanted me to begin writing again. I'd not written much of anything after leaving Coral Ridge, and I'd not been online. I was off grid, under the radar, as I should have been, mainly trying to survive, get help, and not screw something else up. But I love to write; it's how I figure out what I think. And that interior sense that I could and even should write again was exciting. Yet it wasn't a sense that God wanted me to write about whatever I chose, but that God had something specific in mind, that God wanted me to write my story, to tell the painful truth about myself. Specifically, to show the ways in which his mercy and grace stubbornly met me time and time again in my darkest places. I actually had zero interest in writing about anything else. I knew there would have to be a level of transparent honesty about my own secrets and struggles that would be uncomfortable for me. But that was necessary to my path going forward—for me to heal out loud, for me to become real, and help others along the way. In order to show the best parts of God, I knew I had to show the worst parts of me.

"Real isn't how you are made," said the Skin Horse. "It's a thing that happens to you. When a child loves you for a long, long time, not just to play with, but REALLY loves you, then you become Real."

"Does it hurt?" asked the Rabbit.

"Sometimes," said the Skin Horse, for he was always truthful. "When you are Real you don't mind being hurt."

"Does it happen all at once, like being wound up," he asked, "or bit by bit?"

"It doesn't happen all at once," said the Skin Horse. "You become. It takes a long time. That's why it doesn't happen often to people who break easily, or have sharp edges, or who have to be carefully kept. Generally, by the time you are Real, most of your hair has been loved off, and your eyes drop out and you get loose in the joints and very shabby. But these things don't matter at all, because once you are Real you can't be ugly, except to people who don't understand."

—Margery Williams Bianco, *The Velveteen Rabbit*

Isn't that beautiful? I love that. And if I were a different kind of person, I would liken myself to the Velveteen Rabbit. But that's not me, and that's not the softer, poetic approach to writing I felt God was asking of me. Remember, I'm South Florida, man; it's my poetry. So, if I had to describe the writing stance I felt called to, I'd have to nod toward my friend Nadia Bolz-Weber. She captures it best in an interview in which she said:

> When I'm asked why I share so openly about my struggles, I say, "I hope that by being honest I can create a space around me others can step into and feel safer admitting things about themselves." It's a form of leadership I call "Screw it, I'll go first."[42]

Screw it, I'll go first. I'm not sure what Skin Horse would say about that, but there you go.

A friend of mine offered to build a website for me so that I would have a place to publish what I had been recently writing. Not long after we arrived in Florida, my friend finished the site, and I started posting some of the pieces I had written. My gut told me as soon as I stuck my head out a little in public, that it would draw the attention of those who were convinced I should never speak or write publicly again, that my failures had forever disqualified me from doing so. My gut was right, and for a while the winds of opposition blew strong against me, and against Stacie and Living Faith.

We weathered that storm, waiting for it to pass, and like all storms it eventually did. And strangely enough, when those winds died down, I was bombarded by people all over the world telling me their own stories—things they were facing currently, things they were just coming out of, things they were heading into. I have to tell you, it was a little crazy, but also a lot confirming that "Screw it, I'll go first" does indeed create a space where people can feel safe admitting their own screwups. But here's the deal—somebody always has to go first. What's sad and tragic to me is that the way we so often treat people who blow it big (and small) scares others away from telling the truth about themselves.

I wanted to change that. Still do. So, screw it, I'll go first.

A BRIEF SAMPLING

What follows is a brief sampling of the kinds of correspondence I received after I "went first." For each note you read, there are dozens more. All of them heart cries from the fallen, some of them convinced they might never get back up, many trying to put the pieces back together, all of them wondering if the people around them, and that includes God, still love them.

> **Message**: *I wanted to say thank you for being willing to tell your story, share your pain and provide hope to others by allowing us to see God's redemption and restoration in your own life. I came across your article, "Being Kicked Into Freedom," a few weeks ago and by the time I finished reading it, I was sobbing uncontrollably. For the first time in two and a half years, I read the words of someone who expressed exactly what I was feeling and who understood what I was experiencing in a way no one else could.*
>
> *I was a lead pastor for fifteen years. I had the degrees. I was leading a church that was growing rapidly and having an impact in the community, a wife and two sons that I adored. I had it all, until I blew up my life and theirs. Secretly, I'd developed an addiction to pornography that escalated into*

multiple affairs over a two-year period. In 2020, all my sin that I had kept in the darkness was brought to light. I was exposed.

By God's grace, my family is still intact. My wife chose to stay. I am so thankful for that. But I have lost everything else. I've lost the ministry God called me to. I've lost almost all my friends. I've lost all our savings. I've lost my sense of purpose.

Even though my wife and I have worked through the issues that led to my failure and are experiencing relational healing, we feel like a ship without a port. Nothing feels like home anymore. And I personally feel lost. I don't know who I am. It feels like I've lost my purpose. I wonder if I will ever experience joy again. I struggle to find hope for the present and the future. I'm in a job that I hate and am failing in. I know in my head that God is not punishing me, but in my heart, it feels like punishment. I feel like David in Psalm 13, when he cries out, "How long, Lord? Will you forget me forever? How long will you hide your face from me? How long must I wrestle with my thoughts and day after day have sorrow in my heart? How long will my enemy triumph over me?"

Message: *I pastor a small church and was asked to pray a few years ago at the National Day of Prayer in our small town. I was tasked with praying for churches and the gist of my prayer was that pastors would quit being so worried about their reputation. Since then, I wish I hadn't prayed for that. It's been a difficult few years for us. Difficulty in marriage, difficulty with children, difficulty with finances, difficulty in ministry etc. I feel like I know you though we've never met. Rarely a day goes by that I don't feel like a complete failure. I just wanted to encourage you: don't back down. Keep speaking for all the other* *failures out here who aren't perfect and who don't have much of a platform. It's honestly encouraging to hear from someone else who doesn't have that illusion of greatness and I know there are many of us still scared, who are encouraged by your ministry. Keep it up.*

Message: *I'm a middle-aged woman with three children. I've been married nineteen years. Brought up in a very conservative family, I always wanted to follow Jesus. I was always very, very afraid that I didn't do the right thing. I always wanted to put God first. I was very religious. I knew about grace, but I didn't live it.*

I learned about living unafraid of God, but in my heart I always felt the pressure: you are not good enough. You need to do more. I had a lot of mental health issues. I often felt depressed.

Things were becoming a lot better at the time my oldest child was born. But two years later, we lost our second baby just after birth.

I didn't know how to mourn. In this sad circumstance, I read and thought a lot about how to act in times of loss. I was so confused—broken. After several years God gave us another beautiful baby.

After her birth, I was so depressed I couldn't sleep anymore. Long story short: I went to a counselor and we fell in love and began an affair. He's also married.

I know it is so wrong, he also knows it. We didn't want to hurt anybody and up until then I'd always been faithful to my husband. But we also couldn't stop it.

I don't know what to do. I know if we are found out, people will be very angry and sad. But what scares me most is hurting my kids. I can't do that. A divorce would be too hurtful for them! That's the only reason I don't want to tell anybody.

What can I do? I'm losing my hope, my faith, I am so very sad and afraid. How can I live with this guilt until the day I'm bold enough to tell my husband?

Message: *Good morning. I am struggling in the same way that you describe in your article "being kicked into freedom." I was in ministry for twenty years. I turned to alcohol and committed adultery. I was a broken mess when I left the church I was serving. I felt discarded like a piece of trash. The abuse was real, but I find myself using that for self-justification. I want to see myself as more than my failures. So many Christians want to heap on the guilt and shame. I'm having a hard time finding the balance between not justifying my sin and fending off toxic guilt and shame. When things come into the light it's good—but people use it to hammer you, especially in the church! I feel like a man without a country.*

Message: *I very much appreciated your post today about where you were in 2015. I'm there right now. I had an affair in the context of a horrible marriage. But the affair is all that will ever be remembered. I've been bitter and angry towards God.*

At some point, I'll have to sort through my trash and start finding my way back to God. And then I'll have to figure out how to put my life back together. I need help and don't know where to turn.

Message: *I heard you speak at a conference years ago and I'll never forget your message. Tonight, I found the notes I took. I decided to look you up and never thought I'd find what I did. Your posts are exactly what I need. In January 2014 I began what would be my first and only ministry position that lasted* *seven years. My life was secretly out of control and to make a very long story short, I not only lost my job but am facing up to thirty-six months in prison.*

Every day I wake up and feel like a failure. Ministry was the only thing I've ever felt truly passionate about and I screwed it up. I'm proud to say that since Feb. 2021 I've been picking up the pieces of what I've broken. I'm surrounded by some amazing people and I'm leaning on God more than ever before. That's all I can do. Relationally I've lost so many people. I'm financially drained. I don't know how anyone could make it without God.

But I just wanted to write to you and thank you for your transparency and I hope one day my life will be restored to a spot where I can use my story to inspire others like you do. God bless you.

Message: *I had been a successful pastor, author, and denominational leader for thirty-five years. My son-in-law discovered my sinful "history" on my computer that included pornographic websites and same-sex chat room conversations. He reported it to my wife, family, and church. My wife left the next day and filed for divorce, my children have never spoken to me again, and the denomination expelled me, removing my license and credentials. I've lost my marriage, family, church, reputation, friends, and all my colleagues. I'm now alone, fifteen months later, in an apartment by myself, clinging to Jesus, grateful for his forgiveness and mercy, but devastated by the consequences of my decisions. Please pray for me as I try to move forward by His grace. Thanks for listening! God bless you!*

Message: *I was working full-time at a recovery place. I cheated on my husband and wasn't caught but I confessed it. I have since been cast out by everyone. I am hopeless and don't know* *what to do. I've lost my husband, my job, my friends, everything. Most days I feel like I have lost God too. I want to believe that he loves me and hasn't given up on me, but it sure feels like he has. I need help. I need hope. I don't know where to turn. After reading your story I felt like you'd be able to understand what I'm going through without judging me.*

A PLACE WHERE...

From time to time you hear people say, "Church is not a place, it's the people." It's usually said where there's an overemphasis on buildings and property and programs and people getting upset because someone sat in "their seat." That kind of stuff is ridiculous, and exhausting. However, there's an opposite but equal exhaustion that comes from those de-emphasizing the physical place where people gather. Unless you're some kind of disembodied soul floating above our heads, your worship and your community will happen in a specific place on this specific planet. Whether it's a cathedral or a school auditorium or a coffee house or your back deck is beside the point. The point is, we all need a place. We all need people. Stacie and I certainly did. And for that season, God knew that the place and people we needed was Living Faith. So in 2017, Stacie and I joined that church, officially became members and submitted ourselves to the love and oversight of that congregation—taking what the ancient church called "vows of stability." Living Faith became our stable sanctuary.

And due to the ways in which grace had been cultivated there for over twenty years with Pat Thurmer as pastor, Living Faith was a place where sin doesn't shock, and grace still amazes. That church, those people took it on the chin for us, especially Pat. Pat and the leadership of Living Faith were mercilessly attacked by complete strangers, and even some from inside their own ranks, simply for welcoming us into their community.

Imagine a church being blasted for welcoming a sinner whose sins were well known and yet who *wants* to be in church? Flannery O'Connor once perceptively wrote, "The operation of the church is entirely set up for the sinner; which creates much misunderstanding among the smug."[43] So, I guess that stuff shouldn't surprise me anymore, but it's still baffling. And sad. It calls to mind the words from Paul Zahl I shared earlier that "the Church is almost 99.9% of the time unable to apply its greatest gift to the sinner. When it comes to grace, God's people choke."

BLOOD SPORT

That's what I call it. You probably know it by the phrase "cancel culture." And while there have been instances where "canceling" led to justice and liberty for some, more often than not, in my opinion, it's like blood sport.

The phrase *cancel culture* refers to the practice of withdrawing support for (or canceling) people—usually public figures—after they have done or said something destructive, distasteful, or morally disagreeable. We've seen this in recent years with famous people such as Mel Gibson, J K Rowling, Lance Armstrong, Johnny Depp, Dave Chappelle, Will Smith, Taylor Swift, Kanye West, and Roseanne Barr, just to name a few. And when you think about it, cancel culture's not going anywhere because it's always been around. But what in our past was a rather small, local phenomenon—like rounding up the ogre in the swamp—we now live with on the Internet, and the entire world's a stage to be acted upon, and sadly sometimes, crucified on. We are now living, in the words of Philip Yancey, in "an atmosphere choked with the fumes of ungrace."[44]

As I write this book, everybody from politicians to pastors, actors to athletes, comedians to commentators, artists to activists, and singers to statues have and are being socially "canceled" based on the wrong tweet, the wrong tone, the wrong opinion, the wrong decision, the wrong word, the wrong anything. In some cases, "dirt" from twenty years ago (or two hundred years ago!) is being dug up and re-revealed for the world to see. There's no statute of limitations.

And while we've seen this happen primarily with well-known people who have done harmful or objectionable things, we also experience it in our own lives. At some level we have all felt the pain and shame of being written off based on things we have done or failed to do. We've all been unfriended, dismissed, rejected, cast out. We've all felt canceled by someone.

But we've also canceled others.

We tend to remember people primarily by the scandalous things they've done or the specific ways we were once hurt by them. And therefore, from our vantage point, that's who they are fully and finally. They are beyond the scope of redemption, at least to us. They get no quarter, no clemency, no grace from us. In "cancel culture," any failure renders a final verdict: banned for life.

Our countercultural Savior, however, will have none of it.

Jesus had a word for "canceled" people: *friends*. In fact, his circle of followers included a betrayer, a thief, and a prostitute, just to name a few. He was unwilling to "cancel" the worst of the worst, the baddest of the bad, and the guiltiest of the guilty. He moved toward those whom society moved away from. Like I said earlier, he befriended, loved, and touched the outcast, the misfit, the leper, the liar, the sexually deviant. He refused to dismiss those who had been dismissed, reject those who had been rejected, denounce those who had been denounced, and shame those who had been shamed. In fact, his closest friends were of such ill-repute that the religious leaders concluded Jesus must be an imposter because no self-respecting man of God would embrace the kinds of people Jesus embraced.

There is one kind of canceling, however, that Jesus was all about. Colossians 2:13–14 says, "He forgave us all our sins, having canceled the charge of our legal indebtedness, which stood against us and condemned us; he has taken it away, nailing it to the cross" (NIV).

Maybe this is the reason why Jesus himself was canceled by his culture and honestly continues to be canceled by ours. The scandal of his promiscuous love toward those who are hated—his amazing grace to those who are guilty—is just too vulgar for a culture that must find some solace in dealing with the uncomfortable log in their own eye by pointing out the speck in someone else's. "Our drug of choice these days," tweeted Nadia Bolz-Weber, "seems to be knowing who we're better than."

That's the big difference between Jesus and cancel culture: while our culture (including the church) cancels people who have done terrible things, Jesus cancels the terrible things that people are canceled for. The sins and scandals that cancel culture chooses not to forget, Jesus chooses not to remember. What he does remember, and never forgets, is that he is the friend of sinners, the brother of the outcast, and the God of seventy-times-seven forgiveness.

Sadly, cancel culture has made it quite clear that disclosing your sins and shadows, even in a supposedly safe space like "church," can be dangerous. The consequences are too dire, the stakes are too high. You could end up losing friends, followers, opportunities, your career. So, many people wrestling with God-knows-what continue to hide and struggle silently, hoping no one ever discovers their secrets. And we all have them. Every one of us has something in our lives which, if it were exposed, would cause us to contemplate suicide.

But our Living Faith family and Pat Thurmer, in particular, were the beautiful exception to the rule of blood sporting that is all too common. They didn't budge. They didn't blink. They were steadfast. They poured their courage into us; in other words, they en-couraged us. The word *courage* comes from the French *cuer* meaning "heart." Living Faith Church, this tiny Lutheran congregation on the southwest coast of Florida filled with aging Midwesterners, strengthened our hearts. And as for Saint Patrick Thurmer, well, he is simply a wonder of wonders–what every pastor ought to be. It's grace, always grace with that guy. Damn, I love him.

The world is in dire need of communities like Living Faith— communities where those who have failed find God's forgiveness because God's forgiveness has found us; communities that stick with people as they stumble through the difficulties of life the way God sticks with us; communities that exercise outrageous grace—the kind of grace that refuses to give up on those trapped by sin the way God refuses to give up on us.

"It takes a village . . ."

If you've heard that proverb before, then you no doubt know the second half—"to raise a child." I agree with that. Yet I am also a witness to the reality that to heal a heart, it takes a community (and maybe two). What kind of community? Well, one or more with those twin streams of grace and truth as their life's blood. After that, the sign outside could read Caney Creek Cowboy Church or Living Faith Lutheran Church or Lake Wobegon's Our Lady of Perpetual Responsibility. How do I know this for sure? All I have is my story, the one God has called me to speak and write, and from what I've seen with my eyes and heard with my ears and sensed on my skin, it takes a community to heal a heart.

P. S. - HOW LONG?

I said I'd come back to this. So, a postscript to this chapter concerning the element of time, specifically regarding questions like: *How long should I have waited until writing again in a public way? How long did I need to wait before I preached a sermon again? How long does a fallen pastor heal before returning to the role of pastor?*

The spring of 1996 proved one of the most disastrous seasons in the climbing history of Mount Everest. Most of those who have a sense of that story (over twenty-five years ago now) do so due to journalist and climber Jon Krakauer's harrowing account in *Outside* magazine, and later his best-selling book, *Into Thin Air*, based on that account. Krakauer was a member of the expedition that May, and by the time he returned to Base Camp after summitting, nine people from four expeditions were dead, and three more would die before the end of that month. The expedition left Krakauer badly shaken. Nevertheless, five weeks after he returned from Nepal, he delivered a manuscript to *Outside*, and the 17,000-word article was published in the September issue of the magazine. You read that right, five weeks.

I found these paragraphs from Krakauer's book telling when considering questions of *how long?*:

> Several authors and editors I respect counseled me not to write the book as quickly as I did; they urged me to wait two or three years and put some distance between me and the expedition in order to gain some crucial perspective.

Their advice was sound, but in the end I ignored it—
mostly because what happened on the mountain was
gnawing my guts out. I thought that writing the book
might purge Everest from my life.

It hasn't, of course. Moreover, I agree that readers
are often poorly served when an author writes as an act
of catharsis, as I have done here. But I hoped something
would be gained by spilling my soul in the calamity's
immediate aftermath, in the roil and torment of the
moment. I wanted my account to have a raw, ruthless
sort of honesty that seemed in danger of leaching away
with the passage of time and the dissipation of anguish.

Some of the same people who warned me against
writing hastily had also cautioned me against going to
Everest in the first place. There were many, many fine
reasons not to go, but attempting to climb Everest is
an intrinsically irrational act—a triumph of desire over
sensibility. Any person who would seriously consider
it is almost by definition beyond the sway of reasoned
argument.[45]

I can't place my story on top of Krakauer's; they don't line up;
there are far too many differences. But there are a couple of places
where the narratives converge, or at least overlap. Krakauer turned
in a manuscript in five weeks whereas I waited two years before
writing for a wide audience. But we both felt a certain kind of raw
honesty could be lost with the passage of time, that something was
to be gained by writing in "the immediate aftermath." Mine was a
little less immediate, but it was still not long after. I still believe that
not waiting too long is important, and looking back over the volume

of responses I received after I started writing again only steadies my still-at-times-shaky resolve. I could have waited longer; some would say I should have. But in the end, I didn't.

And then there's Krakauer's hope that the writing might somehow "purge" Everest from his life and that maybe he could move on, get on with living. I have also thought, hoped even, that writing about my destructive behavior and indelible regrets would purge me of them somehow, and then I could move on too. I'm not talking about forgiveness here as I believe God has forgiven me fully and completely. And my life has moved on in some very obvious ways. But I'm more talking about coming to some sort of peace within myself about the people I hurt, and the things I did. To this day, Krakauer remains haunted by his demons. I don't know if I would use the word *haunted*, but to say I've been purged of them, that they're not somehow crouching at the door, always lurking about? That would be an outright lie.

Chapter 9
HEALED BUT NOT WHOLE

It was the still-living membership of his friends who, with Flora and their children and their place, pieced Andy together and made him finally well again after he lost his right hand to a harvesting machine in the fall of 1974 . . . . He was forty then, too old to make easily a new start, though his life could be continued only by a new start. He had no other choice.

—Wendell Berry, "Dismemberment"

So begins one of Wendell Berry's short stories about Andy Catlett, a member of the Port William community that Berry has so richly illustrated over a lifetime of writings. "Dismemberment" begins telling of Andy's accident, that of losing his right hand when he attempted to unclog the corn picker without stopping it. He knew better than to not stop it, but he did it anyway. Hmmm, now sounds familiar, doesn't it? Andy's *own damn fault*. Losing his right hand was a monumental loss, it rendered him unable to perform the work that gave shape and form to his life on the land. He would never be the same again, never *right*.

His life had been deformed. His hand was gone, his right hand that had been his principal connection to the world, and the absence of it could not be repaired. The only remedy was to re-form his life around his loss, as a tree grows live wood over its scars. From the memory and a sort of foreknowledge of wholeness, after he had grown sick enough finally of his grieving over himself, he chose to heal.[46]

The rest of the story is a gradual unfolding of Andy getting "better." There's a poignant scene where Andy's neighbors come to help him with his first cutting of hay. There's no way Andy could do the work, much less complete it, and his neighbors know this and come to help even though Andy, in his selfishness, couldn't bring himself to ask for their help. He needed them, and they came. Andy's neighbors—his friends—involve him in the day's work not by overemphasizing his dis-ability yet not ignoring it either. They "moved him to the margin of his difficulty, and his self-absorption. They made him one with them."[47] When the job is finished, Andy fumbles with knowing what to say, how to accurately express his gratitude. One of his friends, Nathan Coulter, reaches out to grab Andy's right forearm, the stump, the site of Andy's un-rightness.

Nathan gripped the hurt, the estranged arm of his friend and kinsman as if it were the commonest, most familiar object around. He looked straight at Andy and gave a little laugh. He said, "Help *us*." After that Andy was one of them. He was better.[48]

Andy continues getting "better." In addition to the farm work, Andy writes of things agricultural, and his writings draw attention. He is invited to speak at gatherings, so he begins to travel a bit, and on one of those trips he experiences a sudden awareness of his life's riches—the gifts of wife and children, true-blue friends and neighbors, pets and livestock, the good land. Andy sees his smallness in the big picture, how he fits in the frame, that "his life is not his own." The resulting emotion is joy, what I'd call a *laughing heart*.

He became, containing his losses, healed, though never again would he be whole.[49]

I'll come back to that sentence shortly because it's vitally important, but more because it's true.

CONTINUING EDUCATION

I mentioned that a friend built a website for me and that I began writing again. I wouldn't say there was a plan to any of it beyond being as honest as I could about where I'd been and where I was at the moment. I still couldn't see very far ahead. The writing, as often writers attest to, served as a medium for me to wrestle with my thoughts and feelings, and occasionally figure out a thing or two. People began responding to what I wrote, and some of those responses turned into invitations to come and speak. I was invited to speak at churches, prisons, recovery centers, retreats, conferences, and colleges. I wasn't choosy when invitations arrived. For one thing, I couldn't afford to be, but more importantly because I didn't desire to live that way going forward. And as I've learned, there is no going back; there is only going forward, going to.

The traveling season—that's what we call it, and I say *we* because Stacie went with me, every time, every invitation. We also saw it as in-person continuing education. We visited so many slices of the American religious denominational pie, from an 8,000 member African American church to a predominantly white Presbyterian congregation of 30 people meeting in a middle school cafeteria. I spoke at nondenominational churches, Baptist churches, Assemblies of God churches, an Episcopalian church, a Cowboy church, and a Lutheran church. We traveled to Michigan, Georgia, Texas, Tennessee, Ohio, Utah, North Carolina, New Jersey, California, Mississippi, New York, and Brazil, just to name a few. While exhausting (many times traveling three weekends out of every month), that season healed me, healed us, in ways I can only see in retrospect. In our travels, Stacie and I shared in a ton of conversations around church life—what seemed to be working, what wasn't, what *church* ought to be/mean—all fodder for the personal conversations we'd been having for a couple of years about a place we one day hoped to be a part of, a place where people could gather and be bracingly honest about the losses and struggles. We didn't know if that place would be a church, a retreat center, a recovery place, or a little bit of all three. But we had lively conversations about this thing called "the church." One of those conversations had to do with what should be the unwavering message, one that it took great grief to remind me of.

The morning of February 21, 2018, was the morning my grandfather died. It seems like it was yesterday, which is a cliche thing to say, but it's true. Even though we had been anticipating his death for quite some time, it was still a shock. Regardless of age or cause, death is always jolting and painful. It is, after all, *"the last enemy"* (1 Corinthians 15:26). Or as the poets say, "the old sorrow."

My grandfather was William Franklin Graham Jr., better known as Billy Graham, the world-renowned preacher and spiritual leader and personal counselor to every American president since Harry S. Truman. He was 99 years old, and even though Parkinson's disease greatly altered his later years, his presence in this world and in my life steadied me. The world knew him as Billy Graham, but to me he was Daddy Bill.

As I sat on the edge of the bed, numbness swallowed me. The finality of his death hit me hard. While my phone kept buzzing with calls and text messages from people sending me their condolences, all I could think about was how this was the first time since I came into this world in 1972 that I would no longer have access to Daddy Bill. In this life, I would never again be able to talk with him, seek his counsel, hear his prayers for me, listen to his stories, laugh at his idiosyncrasies, or go on walks and swim with him. For my entire life he was a loving source of strength and comfort and support and guidance. He was there for me during all my ups and downs. I told my mom that even though in his later years he wasn't the same, just knowing he was there—one phone call or plane ride away—was reassuring to me. It gave me a deep peace. And now he was gone.

I sat in stunned silence for a while until I finally mustered up the wherewithal to get up and turn on the TV. That's when the tears began to flow. Tributes from people all over the world were rolling in. People from all walks of life, religious backgrounds, and political persuasions spoke glowingly of my granddad's life and global impact. It was clear that my family and I weren't the only ones grieving his death. The world was grieving the loss of his trustworthy stature, his unifying influence, his robust integrity, and his respected perspective. He was once called "America's Pastor" for a reason.

But as important and remarkable as all those tributes were, as important and remarkable as he himself was, I was simply missing my granddad. More tears began to flow as I pondered the fact that the hands that gripped so many pulpits held me as a baby. The voice that boomed the truths of the Gospel spoke gently to me as a child. The man who prayed alongside multiple presidents took my hand and prayed with me. Whatever great things were said about Billy Graham, the greatest thing about him to me was that he loved me unconditionally.

As I sat there, I vividly remembered a night when I was in college many years ago. On that night I got down on the floor—face down—and begged God to make me into a man like my granddad. I asked God to keep me humble like him, to make me a man of integrity like him, to develop the same kind of character in me that he developed in him. God's call put my granddad's feet on a path from which he never wavered. And he fulfilled that calling without ever being guilty of any sexual, financial, or other moral scandal. I wanted to be just like him when I grew up.

It was amazingly sweet for me to listen to and read all the tributes that came in, but they were also a sour reminder of how *not* like Daddy Bill I had become. I failed to become like him when I grew up. If my grandfather's moral steadfastness was legendary, mine was equally legendary but in the opposite direction. Having myself been entrusted with a call to deliver the good news of God's boundless love to a broken world, I blew it. I had it all: the influence, the gifts, the charisma, the platform, and the audience. As I've said, I screwed up.

A couple of nights after Daddy Bill's death, I sent this note to a friend:

> Watching my grandfather's life, it has hit me afresh just how selfish and arrogant I was, how much I squandered. And for what? For **what**? What does it profit a man to gain the world and lose his soul? Character matters. It does not gain us favor with God, but it does give us credibility with others so that we can deliver God's favor to the world. I blew it. I'm undone.

My friend responded with six words:

> There was a man named David.

And I lost it.

Calvin says that God takes an aesthetic pleasure in people. There's no reason to imagine that God would choose to surround himself into infinite time with people whose only distinction is that they fail to transgress. King David, for example, was up to a lot of no good. To think only faultless people are worthwhile seems like an incredible exclusion of almost everything of deep value in the human saga.

—Marilynne Robinson

Unlike Daddy Bill, I screwed up. And there is no going back. But I believe that if Daddy Bill were still alive, he'd say something like this to me:

Tullian, I may not be guilty externally of the same sins you are, but I assure you that my heart is no less sinful than yours. According to God's standard of perfection, I'm a failure just like you. All of our records are stained with sin. But the good news of God's grace is that Jesus' perfect record is ours by faith. When God looks at our account, he doesn't see all of our nasty withdrawals. Rather, he sees all of Jesus' perfect deposits. In fact, God doesn't even remember your sins. So, take heart, failed one. Before God, you're loved and accepted and clean.

And Tullian? I love you.

So, for me, for you, for each of us, there is no going back to a past that we have lost or screwed up or outright destroyed. There is no going back and expunging our blemished record or deleting our history. But there is a going *to*: going to the God who has forgiven and forgotten the sins of our yesterdays, todays, and tomorrows; the God who continues to liberate us from ourselves and who reminds us that despite our past, he has promised us a future; the God who won't stop pursuing us, no matter how far or how fast we run; the God who has already welcomed us, accepted us, and given us a new record and a new name: *Beloved.*

That was Daddy Bill's one sermon. He lived it in person and preached it from the pulpit. That truth was his comfort in life and death, as it is mine. Have I failed to live up to my grandfather's standards? In one sense, sure. But releasing ourselves and our families of origin from unreasonable expectations is a smart move. Not easy, but smart. Doing so allows you and them the freedom to be who they actually are. The operative word there is *freedom.* The grace Daddy Bill preached was all about freedom—a message meant to liberate, not further burden, a proclamation of the only hope for a lost and broken world full of lost and broken people; namely, the love of God.

WHAT WE THINK ABOUT WHEN WE THINK ABOUT CHURCH

> But I love my church. It is a humble place—no limestone cathedral, no basilica. It doesn't even have the name of a saint. It has the name of my present obsession. Holy Incarnation was founded to care for the most destitute people in the city, the cast-asides, the no-goods, the impossible, the toxic and contaminated. It is a small glass and brick and cinder-block place with no convenient parking. It is very different from the exurb Protestant churches that I have also attended, with their vast asphalted lot, their vaults of stone and cement, their jumbotrons up front to show close-ups of the minister. Mine is not a church of the saved, but a church of the lost.
>
> —Louise Erdrich, *Future Home of the Living God*

In one of those traveling-season-continuing-education weekends, Stacie and I found ourselves sitting, waiting in DFW airport, feeling simultaneously energized and exhausted. This was November 2018. And Stacie's phone rang. A childhood friend of mine who had met Stacie a few years earlier called to ask if we'd ever consider starting a church, and if so, would we be willing to come visit with a group of interested people. Now I'd started a church back in my early thirties and that experience wore me completely out. To step back into a similar experience now in my late forties gave me pause because in many ways, church planting is a young man's game. But I was so tired of being on the road that church-planting exhaustion momentarily paled in comparison to constant-traveling exhaustion, so I paused, at least intrigued by my friend's phone call if for nothing else than it might mean being able to get off the road and be in one place. And that place just happened to be Jupiter, Florida, a beautiful beach town back on the southeast coast, about forty-five minutes north of Fort Lauderdale where home had always been, where my kids and grandkids lived, and where I longed to be.

When I say the prospect of church planting kicked up exhaustion in me, there's more to it than just that. Do you remember as a kid barreling down the street on your bike or skateboard, and then crashing and burning? The result (in addition to possible broken bones, missing teeth, the inability to remember your name for a few minutes) was always varying degrees of road rash. Just four years earlier I had crashed and burned within the context of *church*. The result? Church rash. So, the thought of entrusting my life and livelihood into the hands of Christians again? Yeah, I was like *Oh, hell no.* In my experience, Christians tend to bail when the shit hits the fan, when life gets messy. Based on that I was extremely reticent about trusting any group of Christians with my heart and life along with the hearts and lives of the ones I love most. Now we'd had beautiful experiences at Caney Creek and Living Faith, but I'd not been the pastor or leader in those situations. A pastor crashing and burning comes with its own brand of church rash, and mine still felt raw.

Stacie and I talked, and we decided to at least meet with these people. But I felt it was imperative that I tell my story—unedited, as honest as possible without being unnecessarily shocking. I was going to tell the truth about myself. And if, after hearing my story, these people were still interested in talking further with us about starting and leading a church, well then maybe there's something going on here. And if not, then there's clearly not. I know that phrase, "telling the truth about ourselves," is heard a lot in church culture, but my experience has been that for the most part, we don't. We might a little, but there's usually an unspoken "flat-earth theory" when it comes to God's (and people's) grace. There's an edge or horizon, and if you sail beyond that—tell too much truth—you'll fall off. I believe God's grace has no edge; it goes round and round. And so, I believe the church should be the safest place to tell the truth, the whole truth, and nothing but the truth, so help me God, about ourselves. But all too often, it's the scariest.

William Inge's 1971 novel *My Son Is a Splendid Driver* anguishingly illustrates this typical "unsafeness." The narrator, a man in his mid-forties, is visiting his parents for Christmas. His parents still live in the small Kansas town where he grew up. Uncharacteristically, his mother is not there to meet him at the train station (the novel is set during the Great Depression). When he arrives at his home, his mother is there, but she's extremely thin and looks worn. She's about sixty-six years old. She gets right to the point:

> "Why do you suppose I didn't go to the depot. I always do, don't I? . . . I didn't go this time because I'm ashamed to be seen." Then she posed her face before me

under the light, and I saw a couple of raw little sores on her lower lip, supposing them to be fever blisters.

"Your father has given me a disease that I don't have the courage to name."[50]

The narrator's father has given his mother an STD that he contracted from a prostitute during a business trip away from home. William Inge then reflects on what the son has just heard:

Mother had stopped going to church. "Church is just a place to go when you're feeling good and have a new hat to wear." There was a little bitterness in what she said, but there was also truth. Our minister would have been the last person in the world she could have talked to, to have lifted the curse she felt upon her and saved her from feeling damned. She would have embarrassed the man into speechlessness had she gone to him with her story. He would have been unable to look at her or my father without coloring. Most of our morality, I was beginning to think, was based on a refusal to recognize sin. Our entire religious heritage, it seemed to me, was one of refusal to deal with it.[51]

Telling the truth about yourself is a stance against the refusal to recognize sin, the refusal to deal with it. Telling the truth about yourself is the only basket worth putting your eggs in. But the only way for "the courage to name" to be born is to know how much God loves you. You will be able to talk truthfully about your worst, most embarrassing, most shameful parts with less fear when you know that the only person's approval you ultimately need is God's and that you already have it. As I said earlier, those who are most free are those who have the least fear telling the truth about themselves. And those who have the least fear telling the truth about themselves are those who know how unconditionally loved they are by God. That message, and that message alone, is what matters to me.

So, in February of 2019, we made the two-hour drive from Fort Myers to Jupiter, Florida, and met with about thirty people in the common room of a country club. I shared; Stacie shared; we put all our cards on the table. We shared that in light of our stories and in light of what we believe about God's grace, if we were to ever even consider starting anything, it would be a recovery place masquerading as a church. Guess what? They invited us back for another weekend, and this time they asked me to preach. Two weeks later, we drove back to Jupiter and spent the weekend with this group of people and repeated that same weekend-preaching-visit two weeks later. By this time the initial thirty had grown to around seventy, and everyone in the room, including Stacie and me, had the sense that this is what we wanted to do. I could have said, "we sensed this is what God wanted us to do," and while I did have that feeling in the days to come, initially it was as much a feeling of God saying, "Okay, try it. I'll be right there with you."

We moved to Jupiter in April, spent that spring and summer laying the groundwork, and in September of 2019, we officially launched The Sanctuary—a recovery place masquerading as a church (in a high school auditorium, where many churches tend to begin).

If you were to read between the lines of that past paragraph, you'd see the birth story of The Sanctuary wasn't anywhere near as smooth as it sounds. There were all the initial challenges of starting something new, and while some people are a fairly blank slate when it comes to church, more often than not, people have an idea (if not ideas) as to what church ought to look like and sound like and feel like. But one of the unsmooth edges of that beginning that continues to "hurt" to this day has to do with Stacie's distance from her home in Texas and the people she loves there. Don't hear me wrong, she was more excited than I was about beginning something new together, but that vitality was tinged with a sadness—she greatly misses her people, and I love that about her. Stacie has often said that God would have to make it crystal clear to her that this was the next step of our journey together. God did for Stacie, and she agreed to taking the step.

For me, it wasn't so crystal clear. At that time, I identified as "the world's most reluctant church planter," yet I agreed as well that what we were doing felt right. Even in our varying degrees of enthusiasm, it was hard for both of us for differing reasons, but it felt right. When asked about his plan for any given day, Brennan Manning would always grin and say, "I'm simply going to do the next thing in love." He cribbed that line from Catherine of Siena, as poets often do. I'm not sure I could say that I was starting The Sanctuary in love. For me, at the time, it felt more like I was starting The Sanctuary to survive. But I did have a deep sense of quiet knowing that this was the next thing.

We met together for about six months, and then COVID shut the world down. Remember that one? Yeah, unforgettable. We thought we might be shut down for two to three weeks at the most. Eight months later, November 2020, we re-launched The Sanctuary, this time in a space we could call our own, and this time with even greater clarity about *what* The Sanctuary is—a place where people can be honest—and *who* The Sanctuary is—a family of misfits fitted together by a misfit God. The *what* and the *who* are grounded in what artist Rich Mullins penned "the reckless raging fury that they call the love of God."[52]

CHRIST OF THE CYCLONE

About two and half hours south of Puerto Vallarta lies the small town of Barra de Navidad, one of Mexico's best-kept secrets. Cobblestone streets lined with tiny markets, authentic Mexican food, and endless stretches of uncrowded beaches make it a popular vacation and retirement destination. But on September 1, 1971, Hurricane Lily blew through bringing massive devastation. The story goes that as people sought sanctuary in the Catholic Church, the effects of the storm caused the arms of Christ on the crucifix to break and hang down at his sides. The moment the arms of Christ broke, the winds stopped, and no lives were lost in Barra. Forty miles south in Manzanillo, 1,500 people met their deaths. Ever since that day, the crucifix has been known as Christ of the Cyclone. There were those who wanted to repair the crucifix, fix it, but the Pope declared no; a miracle had happened there—leave the arms broken.

Leave the arms broken.

I promised I'd come back to this line from Wendell Berry's short story: "He became, containing his losses, healed, though never again would he be whole."[53] I've said that The Sanctuary is a recovery place masquerading as a church, and while that's a bit tongue-in-cheek, it's also very true. But some clarity on "recovery" is needed here; so, I want to address two things.

First. *Recovery* brings to most minds people in recovery programs for things like alcohol or drug abuse, eating disorders, anger management, sexual addiction, those sorts of things. Yet the truth is that we're all in recovery. We've all been hurt and disappointed, we've all experienced the disillusionment of unmet expectations, we all have fears and insecurities, we've all felt unloved and rejected in some way. And therefore, we all have unhealthy relationships with something or someone we depend on to soothe the pain—to make us feel strong, secure, safe, important, loved, in control. We're all attached to something we think we need to be happy and content. Your addiction may not be alcohol, but it may be getting approval. It may not be getting high, but it may be getting respect. It may not be sex, but it may be getting attention for the way you look or for your professional achievements. It may not be food, but it may be financial stability. It may not be nicotine, but it may be feeling important. It may not be social media, but it may be the need to be in control. All of us are drunk on something. All of us need sobriety. So, there are two types of people in the world: people in recovery who know they are and people in recovery who think they're not. But if you're a human, you're recovering. We're all in.

Second. *Recovery*—what Wendell Berry described as "getting better." But there's a chance that could be misleading because most people think "getting better" means "getting fixed." And I completely understand that mindset because it's a seemingly much easier, cleaner, faster approach—hell, that's what I kept doing following all my screwups. I just wanted to find the fix—fix it, fix them, fix us, fix me.

Twice a month, a handful of men from our church get together with no agenda other than to connect and open up about whatever's going on in our lives. It's not your typical "church" group. And we aren't your typical "church" guys. It's more like an AA meeting. We call it "The Vault" because what's said there stays there. Everyone is free and safe to admit areas of helplessness, failure, and frustration. Divorce, addiction, infidelity, financial bankruptcy, suicidal thoughts, childhood trauma, just an overall sense of lostness—these are just some of the issues we come to the table with. There are guys in their twenties and guys in their sixties. There are no rules for what can and can't be said. No restrictions on language—no one bats an eye when someone says "fuck." Nobody lectures anybody. No one gives advice. We listen to one another. Support one another. We laugh. We cry. We sometimes lose our shit. And we come with the understanding that the best thing we can do for each other is to simply be an environment in which, when any of us need to come up for air, we can. No judgement. No correction.

Many people assume that God's grace is missing in action where improvement is lacking. But maybe, just maybe, my willingness to admit my lack of improvement in some ways *is* a sign of improvement. Maybe it's when I stop obsessing over my need to get better and instead acknowledge that I need grace . . . maybe that *is* what it means to get better. In other words, maybe God's grace at work in my life is my growing realization of how much grace I need, or how much grace I already have. Maybe we're looking for God in all the wrong places. Maybe God hangs out in the slums of our weaknesses and fears and failures and insecurities and stubbornness and unbelief rather than in the bustling cities of our strengths and accomplishments and victories and "goodnesses." As C. S. Lewis said, "It is when we notice the dirt that God is most present in us; it is the very sign of his presence."[54]

Remember Paul Zahl, my friend who refused to turn his face away when I was so lost? Remember I told you how he'd always say "stick with that" each time I would pour out the depths of my distress? What he meant was there's much to learn in the place of ruin, much to see at the scene of pain and loss and regret and shame and fear, so don't be too quick to look for a way out, otherwise known as "fix it." Paul knew, and I'm learning, that we tend to make a god out of getting fixed, that we tend to idolize things like progressing beyond hard and bad places and transcending bad qualities, and in the process, we often end up missing something essential. Here's a few *what-ifs?* to chew on. What if real progress is a growing awareness of our need for help, a deepening deconstruction of our burdensome and delusional sense of self-sufficiency? What if true growth isn't about the heights we should attain but about acknowledging the depth of our need? What if "getting better" has more to do with accepting our limitations, finally taking off the masks we wear, and being honest about our "unfixedness"? What if real recovery is marked by a growing acceptance of the fact that we will, in this life anyway, never fully recover, that we can be healed but not whole? What if the idea of "closure" promises more than it can deliver? I mean, we can come close, get in the ballpark, so to speak, keep on living—even thrive. But closure *closure*? Maybe robots, but not flesh and blooders.

Recovery, "getting better," living a life colored by your losses rather than erasing them, is a daily struggle consisting of small beginnings and small steps. It takes a long time—actually a lifetime. We'd prefer it to be linear, so we could track progress and wins, but it's not, not by a long shot. Dr. Patricia Deegan is an adjunct professor at Dartmouth College School of Medicine and an activist in the disability rights movement. In her article "Recovery: The Lived Experience of Rehabilitation," she writes:

> Recovery is a process, a way of life, an attitude,
> and a way of approaching the day's challenges. It is
> not a perfectly linear process. At times our course is

erratic and we falter, slide back, re-group and start again . . . . Recovery is the urge, the wrestle, and the resurrection. Recovery is a matter of rising on *lopped limbs* to a new life. As professionals, we would like nothing more than to somehow manufacture the spirit of recovery and give it to each of our program participants. But this is impossible. We cannot force recovery to happen in our rehabilitation programs. Essential aspects of the recovery process are a matter of grace and, therefore, cannot be willed. However, we can create environments in which the recovery process can be nurtured like a tender and precious seedling. (italics mine)[55]

"Nurtured like a tender and precious seedling" sounds like the way you'd treat a recent amputee, doesn't it? Dr. Deegan's words called to mind another of the messages I receive each week.

Message: *So normally, I don't go around messaging public figures, but after reading your "The Life of an Amputee" post, I'm making an exception.*

I've read a lot of your writings, but this one—wow. I still have tears running down my face from the accuracy of the imagery. This recently divorced pastor's daughter doesn't know if you could've expressed the anguish more powerfully in layman's terms than that.

Thank you for showing up in your brokenness. Broken Christians are nothing new, right? But a willing exposure in the midst of that is a whole different story, something we don't see much. Thank you.

Did you catch her phrase, "the anguish"? She could have chosen any number of words or phrases, but she chose that one. Because pastors' daughters aren't supposed to get divorced, right? Until they do. Kinda like pastors aren't supposed to have multiple affairs, right? Until they do. Kinda like you're not supposed to break things, right? Until you do, or you yourself are broken. That's when you discover where God is. That is, if you know where to look. We've been taught to look up. But if God is *with us*, then . . .

ON THE BATHROOM FLOOR

Her full name is Jane Kristen Marczewski. Fans around the world knew her as Nightbirde. A singer-songwriter, she won the hearts of fans in 2021 with a jaw-dropping performance of her original song "It's OK" on *America's Got Talent*. But back up. In 2017, she was diagnosed with Stage 3 breast cancer. In 2018, she went into remission. In 2019, she opened for Tori Kelly, a "wink from God saying, 'You're good enough to do this, kid.'" Months later she was diagnosed again with a 3- to 6-month life expectancy and a 2% chance of survival. She endured the pandemic and a horrible divorce, and then took a leap of faith to a clinic in Southern California. Nightbirde miraculously recovered. Six months after her diagnosis, she was declared cancer-free. She died on February 19, 2022.

This was her blog entry posted almost a year before her death:

> I have had cancer three times now, and I have barely passed thirty. There are times when I wonder what I must have done to deserve such a story. I fear sometimes that when I die and meet with God, that He will say I disappointed Him, or offended Him, or failed Him.

Maybe He'll say I just never learned the lesson, or that I wasn't grateful enough. But one thing I know for sure is this: *He can never say that He did not know me.*

I am God's downstairs neighbor, banging on the ceiling with a broomstick. I show up at His door every day. Sometimes with songs, sometimes with curses. Sometimes apologies, gifts, questions, demands. Sometimes I use my key under the mat to let myself in. Other times, I sulk outside until He opens the door to me Himself.

I have called Him a cheat and a liar, and I meant it. I have told Him I wanted to die, and I meant it. Tears have become the only prayer I know. Prayers roll over my nostrils and drip down my forearms. They fall to the ground as I reach for Him. These are the prayers I repeat night and day; sunrise, sunset.

Call me bitter if you want to—that's fair. Count me among the angry, the cynical, the offended, the hardened. But count me also among the friends of God. For I have seen Him in rare form. I have felt His exhale, laid in His shadow, squinted to read the message He wrote for me in the grout: "I'm sad too."

If an explanation would help, He would write me one—I know it. But maybe an explanation would only start an argument between us—and I don't want to argue with God. I want to lay in a hammock with Him and trace the veins in His arms.

I remind myself that I'm praying to the God who let the Israelites stay lost for decades. They begged to arrive in the Promised Land, but instead He let them wander, answering prayers they didn't pray. For forty years, their shoes didn't wear out. Fire lit their path each night. Every morning, He sent them mercy-bread from heaven.

I look hard for the answers to the prayers that I didn't pray. I look for the mercy-bread that He promised to bake fresh for me each morning. The Israelites called it *manna*, which means "what is it?"

That's the same question I'm asking—again, and again. There's mercy here somewhere—*but what is it? What is it? What is it?*

I see mercy in the dusty sunlight that outlines the trees, in my mother's crooked hands, in the blanket my friend left for me, in the harmony of the wind chimes. It's not the mercy that I asked for, but it *is* mercy nonetheless. And I learn a new prayer: *thank you*. It's a prayer I don't mean yet, but will repeat until I do . . .

I know it sounds crazy, and I can't really explain it, but God is in there—even now. I have heard it said that some people can't see God because they won't look low enough, and it's true.

If you can't see him, look lower. God is on the bathroom floor.[56]

*   *   *

Our gathering we call The Sanctuary. We're God's downstairs neighbors. We don't have a Christ-of-the-cyclone-esque broken crucifix on the wall, but it wouldn't be a bad idea because that image nails it. We're a bunch of broken people who gather around the God who was broken for us, and we celebrate the miracle of

God's grace, his unconditional love. In the shadow of that love, we willingly expose our brokenness; we "go first." We falter, fail, and begin again. It's really pretty screwed up and beautiful. We've no illusions of being something special, but we strive to be honest about ourselves. We're rising on lopped limbs because of God's great love.

> This urge, wrestle, resurrection of dry sticks . . .
> What saint strained so much,
> Rose on such lopped limbs to a new life?
>
> —Theodore Roethke, "Cuttings"

Epilogue
LIVING AMENDS

We all have regrets and most of us know that those regrets, as excruciating as they can be, are the things that help us lead improved lives. Or, rather, there are certain regrets that, as they emerge, can accompany us on the incremental bettering of our lives. Regrets are forever floating to the surface . . . . They require our attention. You have to do something with them. One way is to seek forgiveness by making what might be called living amends, by using whatever gifts you may have in order to help rehabilitate the world.

—Nick Cave, *Faith, Hope and Carnage*

Yes, that's the quote that started this whole acknowledging the worst parts of me trip you've taken. That acknowledging is never easy. It's embarrassing. For example, every time I stand up in front of a group of people and say that I cheated on my first wife, I cringe. Every time. It sucks to say that in public. Every time I talk about how deceitful I was, I wince inside. Every time. It's extremely uncomfortable admitting that stuff in front of people. When I talk about the hurt I caused my family, my friends, and countless others, I squirm. Disclosing my failures is painfully difficult. I get no rush by confessing those things that I wish no one ever knew about me. It's horribly awkward, every time. I believe I'm forgiven, yet I'm still seeking some sense of forgiveness.

But I don't know a better way to show people the best parts of God than to tell them about some of the worst parts of me. I really believe that it's when we come clean—when we confess our sins, demonstrate our desperation, acknowledge our neediness, tell the truth about our fears and insecurities and struggles and secrets, admit that we are selfish and arrogant and controlling and self-righteous and unforgiving—*that* is when we discover a God who came, not for the righteous but for sinners—a God who graciously rescues and welcomes people who fail because people who fail are all that there are. Trust me, those parts of you that you are most fearful of disclosing—the parts of you that get jealous, the parts of you that are greedy, the parts of you that lust for what you don't have, the parts of you that are scared shitless, the parts of you that thirst for vengeance, the parts of you that are painfully insecure—those are the very parts that will be most helpful to people if you admit them. Opening up about your struggles helps people so much more than talking about your strengths. People may be somewhat inspired when you share your successes with them, but they connect with you (and feel less alone) when you share your failures with them. It gives them hope.

I cannot shake Nick Cave's line: "One way is to seek forgiveness by making what might be called living amends, by using whatever gifts you may have in order to help rehabilitate the world."[57] *Living amends* . . . God, what a phrase. It seems completely counterintuitive to think your failures could be your gifts, but that's what I've found and continue to find. My living amends is honesty

before God and people. But in that honesty, I tell you there are
still days that it doesn't feel like much—like it's not enough, like
it's just noise, some banging away on a drum.

Best known for his novel *The River Why*, David James Duncan's
God Laughs and Plays deserves more attention than it gets. This
book is a collection of essays with the subtitle *Churchless Sermons*,
and, man, do they preach. In one piece, Duncan remembers his
older brother—his best friend—who died at seventeen, when
Duncan was young. As a way to crawl through his grief, he decided
to honor his brother by adopting his brother's habits, likes, and
dislikes, even his tastes in music. But he hit a bump in the adoption
process. His brother's favorite Christmas carol was "The Little
Drummer Boy," and while Duncan started claiming it was his too,
he was lying. But he writes:

> What began to get to me was the song's basic
> premise. Here is some uninvited urchin, standing right
> next to the cradle of a newborn baby, banging away
> on a *drum*. Have any vindictive relatives ever given a
> child in your home a drum? *Pah rum pah pum pum* is
> an extremely kind description of the result. Yet out
> of reverence and love, this unidentified "poor boy"
> marches up to the manger of the (probably sleeping)
> Christ child and bangs the hell out of his drum. The
> more literally I imagined the impropriety of this
> drumming, the more it appealed to me: it spoke to
> the unseemliness of my brother's early death, and to
> Christ's impending death, too. I liked to picture the
> infant Jesus' eyes, so innocent and new that they were
> unable to focus, startling wide O-pen at the sudden
> banging. I liked to picture God the Father, wincing On

High, wanting to cover his beloved son's ears, make the donkey kick the Drummer Boy senseless, send in the Wise Men to stop the banging, only to sigh, swallow His anger and think, "Nope. These are the mortals. This is Earth. This is my beloved son among mortals on Earth. Let the drummer boy drum."[58]

Now, Duncan writes, the first time he hears "The Little Drummer Boy" each December, especially when sung by kids:

The chills run from my spine to my eyes, sometimes spilling over as the truth of the fiction hits home. That it's "a poor boy, too"—same as Jesus, or me, or you: the truth of our spiritual poverty gets to me every time. The line, I played my best for him, pah rum pah pum pum. What more can one offer, no matter how silly or bad it sounds? The line, Then he smiled *at me pah rum pah pum pum*. What more can we hope for . . . ?[59]

Honesty before God and people. That's the gift we honor God with, the drum we bring and bang. What some would call noise, I'd go so far as to call *art*.

TO SING (AGAIN)

I've always loved to sing. I'm not saying I sing well necessarily, but singing has been a bona fide expression for me; I put my entire self into it. But there was a season when I couldn't sing. Well, I could, but just not in church. I wanted to, but I simply couldn't. And I hated that I couldn't. It was during my intense traveling season, when Stacie and I would be gone most weekends for me to guest speak at a church or conference or retreat center. The experience was a bit all over the map, but one constant was the presence of music prior to my speaking. A worship team would guide the gathered in singing several worship songs as a prelude of sorts to "the message." But in each of those situations, I couldn't join in the singing. It was like a wall had been built in me, and the songs couldn't penetrate it. I heard all the lyrics as cheesy, and the whole experience felt disingenuous. Everyone around me always seemed emotionally connected to what was being sung. I wasn't. At all. Ever. I never made a scene or anything; I'd just sit quietly as most everyone else stood jubilantly, which may have been sort of a scene, I don't know. All I know is I couldn't sing, just couldn't do it. At that time, for me, to sing felt fake.

In the fall of 2018, I was invited to speak at a fundraising event for a church in Belton, Texas, on a Saturday night and then stay over to preach their two morning services on Sunday. During that first service on Sunday, something happened to me, something I wasn't expecting. One of the vocalists on their worship team was an African American gentleman with an angelic voice. There was nothing flashy about this guy, like zero showmanship, but he possessed one of the most tender and sincere faces I've ever seen. I couldn't look away. I hesitate to say his face was "sweet," but the truth is it was—innocent, no guile. Soft, warm, hospitable, and humble. The way I always imagined Jesus' face to be when I was a child. And on that day, for reasons beyond me, this man's countenance plus the lyrics to the song—"Do It Again"—well, did it.

> I know the night won't last . . .
> My heart will sing Your praise again.
>
> —"Do It Again," Elevation Worship

The next thing I knew, I was crying. And while I usually sat during the singing portion, I was suddenly standing. Whatever wall that guilt and shame and fear and self-loathing and exhaustion and cynicism had built came tumbling down, and I found myself free to sing again. I realize this sounds a bit out there (and on some level it was), but it was an old-school experience of my heart being strangely warmed, and I seriously couldn't help but stand and sing. So, I did, with my entire self. I was getting better, recovering, rising on lopped limbs to new life.

Some might liken my singing to the drummer boy's banging— noise. But I'd go so far as to humbly call it art.

> Art does have the ability to save us, in so many different ways. It can act as a point of salvation, because it has the potential to put beauty back into the world. And that in itself is a way of making amends, of reconciling us with the world. Art has the power to redress the balance of things, of our wrongs, of our sins . . .
>
> —Nick Cave

THE LAUGHING HEART

I began this memoir with Charles Bukowski's poem, "The Laughing Heart":

> Your life is your life
> Don't let it be clubbed into dank submission.
> Be on the watch.
> There are ways out.
> There is a light somewhere.

It may not be much light but
It beats the darkness.
Be on the watch.
The gods will offer you chances.
Know them.
Take them.
You can't beat death but
You can beat death in life, sometimes.
And the more often you learn to do it,
The more light there will be.
Your life is your life.
Know it while you have it.
You are marvelous
The gods wait to delight
In you.

I initially considered that title—*The Laughing Heart*—for this memoir. But I felt at first glance, whether on a real or online bookshelf, that title, while absolutely true, would be too much too soon. In light of the news cycle bullet point lists of my public failings minus the fuller contents of this book, you probably would have read that title as flippant if not outright disrespectful to those I've hurt deeply. But I've come clean. I've told you what happened. So now, here in the final pages, I make one more confession: I live now with a laughing heart. I didn't say laughing *face*, because the light I now carry doesn't always make it to the surface in "surfacey" ways. I'm talking about something deeper, much deeper . . . a laughter that comes from the wreckage. And while you might not fully believe that "laughing heart" talk is true, my hope is that after all I've shared, you could see it as true enough.

LESS AND MORE

> Catholic theologian James Allison describes faith not as intellectually ascending to a set of theological propositions, but he describes faith as *relaxing*. Relaxing in the love and presence of God in the way we relax in the presence of someone we are certain is fond of us. When we are in the presence of someone we are certain is fond of us, we are funnier, more spontaneous, softer and less defended. If I know for sure someone likes and loves me there is no reason to pretend anything. Allison says faith is relaxing.
>
> —Nadia Bolz-Weber, substack, The Corners, March 15, 2020

The people closest to me say I'm less and more than I used to be. I'm less "what's next?" and more present, less superman (thank God) and more humane, less self-assured and more self-aware, less larger-than-life and more down-to-earth. I'm softer than I used to be; they say "more understanding," more empathetic. My own failures have forced me to reckon with God's forgiveness in a way that has made me more forgiving without even really trying. And as a result, I'm less likely to hold a grudge. I'm far more grateful for the smaller things now. You could say that small things are a big deal to me these days. I take a lot less for granted. People matter more, way more; projects matter less, way less. I'm more of a friend and less of a networker. I enjoy listening more. I love the things that matter most more. Minutes and moments are so much more important to me now. I care way more about today and much less about tomorrow. Life is smaller and slower than it used to be. A lot smaller and much slower. And I love it. It's less grand, less busy, less impressive. I have less stuff, less money, less connections. I'm less celebrated, less influential, and less sought after. And yet, I couldn't care less about all that these days. Because life is slower and smaller, I see more, hear more, feel more. Things are quieter inside me. I'm less distracted. I'm way more content, way more free, and way more comfortable in my own skin. Have I arrived? Ha!—that's funny. No, not by a long shot.

These days I live with a seemingly incurable low-grade fever of sadness because of the people I hurt and some of the relationships I lost. It's the grievous wound of *used to be* that will not heal. I live with lopped off limbs. I still feel like I'm white knuckling it some days—prone to wander, taking destructive detours in my heart. Yes, I'm fully aware of my capacity to screw it all up again, repeating my adulterous history. Lord have mercy. But some place or picture of arrival is not what I'm grasping after. If I'm reaching at all, it is to receive what's been so graciously given—Stacie's love, a family of screwed-up misfit friends, the voices of my children and grandchildren, sunsets and ocean breezes, midnight music festivals with my daughter under the Miami night sky. Poet Maya Popa captures this sentiment perfectly in the title of her book *Wound is the Origin of Wonder*. That it is. And I'm grateful for the wonder that now marks my wounded, rattletrap life. Frederick Buechner famously wrote, "Here is the world. Beautiful and terrible things will happen. Don't be afraid."[60] That's the abundant life, my friends. Experiencing the abundance, all of it, the beautiful and the terrible and everything else in between, every damn stitch, right in the cardia.

* * *

Not long ago I was with a friend at a Rob Zombie, Alice Cooper, Ministry concert (the industrial metal band Ministry—not "ministry" in the way you're probably thinking). My friend is in his late fifties. He's been through a ton of, in his words, "shit-fuckery" over the course of his life. Married three times, two years in jail, strained relationship with his kids, severe PTSD from his military service. I met him a few years ago when I was speaking at a recovery place here in South

Florida (my people!). He was in for alcoholism. He's sober now, and he's wise. His "shit-fuckery" has made him sage-like in his older age. He's reflective now. And I listen to him. He teaches me.

A fully tatted metal-head, he said something to me that night that rang so true, so deep. It was transcendently insightful. And simple.

I asked him how he lives with his regrets. He said:

> The key to my healing has been acceptance. Acceptance of the things I've done, the bridges I've burned, and the relationships I've lost, the no-going-backness. Acceptance of the way life is, rather than the way I want it to be. And in that acceptance, I have found peace and contentment *in* my pain, *in* my regrets, *in* my longings for different outcomes.

A liberatingly powerful and true reminder that God and his grace meets us in our shit-fuckery, not outside of it.

I think, although they might not articulate it exactly in this way, those who know me best would say I've found some measure of peace and contentment *in* acceptance, that as I make my living amends, there's a lightness about me. I can sing again. I've got a laughing heart, one with no reason to pretend any longer, one that only comes by learning to relax "the way we relax in the presence of someone we are certain is fond of us," one that dances to the tune of endless grace—the grace that never ceases to comfort me throughout my carnage-riddled life. A laughing heart has only one beat, that of gratitude. *Thank you.*

*   *   *

For writer Andre Dubus, 1986 was a terrible, horrible, no good, very bad year. In July of that year, life as he knew it completely unraveled. Dubus stopped on a highway to help a woman and her brother who just moments earlier had been in an auto accident. The next thing Dubus knew, a car was barreling toward them. Dubus pushed the woman out of the way, but he and the other man were struck. The man? Killed. Dubus? Severely injured. Dubus suffered thirty-four broken bones; both his legs were crushed. He'd never use his left leg again. And after ten operations, his right leg was amputated just below the knee. Dubus (fifty at the time) would spend the rest of his life in a wheelchair. Yes, a fellow amputee, well acquainted with *used to be*.

Dubus' son, the novelist Andre Dubus III, tells this story in his memoir *Townie*. It was near the end of his father's life (he always called him "Pop"), a season when he and some friends had renovated Pop's house to accommodate his new life in a wheelchair.

Pop had made peace with his crippling. Once, sitting straight in his wheelchair, he'd looked over at me in his small dining room and said, "I'd stop on that highway again. Even knowing what I was going to lose. I would."

"Why?"

"Because I've learned so much."

His father's writing routine continued in that final season, a ritual he'd put in place for himself when he was a young man. He wrote every morning. He'd wheel himself down the hall to his tiny kitchen, pour a cup of tea with honey, balance it on his lap as he'd wheel himself back to his bedroom where he'd sit at his desk and write longhand in pen. His son remembers:

> By midmorning he'd be done. He'd count how many words he'd gotten and record the number. After each total, whether it was fifteen hundred or fifty, he wrote: *Thank you*.[61]

Yes. Thank you.

ACKNOWLEDGMENTS

I've written eight books, but this is my first since 2014. Soon after that book came out, my life came crashing down, and I stopped writing. I didn't have anything to say. I was numb and lifeless for a long time. I needed help. A lot of help. If it weren't for a handful of friends and family members, I wouldn't be here today...and neither would this book.

There are so many people I'd love to thank. I will never forget those who helped me when I was at the end of my rope—when it wasn't popular to be my friend. Most of you know who you are and a thousand thank-you's aren't enough. I'm alive today because of you.

But this book couldn't have, and wouldn't have, been written if it weren't for a few key people.

To my good friend, the incomparable **John Blase**. You worked tirelessly to shape this book from start to finish. You pulled stuff out of me that I would've rather kept concealed. Uncomfortable stuff. Embarrassing stuff. But I'm so glad you did. You held my hand, and often carried me, throughout the whole process. You're the best in the business, hands down. A warrior poet who also served (unwittingly) as my therapist. The way you helped me put words to my feelings and experiences brought about a healing I didn't think possible. So, thank you John. Your friendship, more than this book, is why I believe God brought us together.

To super agents **Greg Johnson** and **Don Pape**. Your belief in me and this project has been constant. The two of you stood by me as non-blinking friends and encouragers when I desperately needed both. Knowing that I wouldn't make you rich and would probably make you unpopular for representing me proves that your friendship is legit. You are gifts to me and to the often-frustrating publishing industry. This book wouldn't be here without your endless hours of help and support. Thank you!

To **Casey Cease, Megan Poling, Carol Jones,** and the team at **Lucid Books**. This is the first book I wrote without having a publisher first. There were a handful of reasons for that. Good ones. But I'm picky. And given the personal nature of this project, I was especially picky. I needed a publisher who wanted to publish this book, not despite the story it tells, but because of it. And in you, I found it. So, thank you. Your bold investment in me and this book proves that you understand the dire need for tales of redemption in this world of retribution.

To **Gabe, Nate,** and **Genna**—my three children. You fill me in ways that are unexplainable. Your one-way love for me when I was at my worst is the greatest demonstration of grace I've ever experienced. I hurt you, and you loved me in return. In so many ways, your uninterrupted love kept me going and brought me back to life. It is the highest privilege to be your dad and to have you as my best friends. I love you.

And to **Stacie**—my wife. I still think you're crazy for falling in love with me, but I thank God all the time that you did. You have cheered me up and cheered me on when I needed it most. You've seen me at my lowest. You've witnessed my breakdowns, my tears, my hopelessness. You've lived through the worst of me and never once turned your back. This book isn't just my story. In so many ways, it is our story. It wouldn't exist without you. And I'm quite sure I wouldn't exist without you either. You are a gift beyond measure, and "I wanna keep on swimming with you" (Le Youth). I love you because I love you.

NOTES

1   Charlotte Brontē, *Villette*, (1858; repr., New York: Penguin Classics, 2004).

2   Mary Karr, *Lit: A Memoir (P.S.)* (New York: Harper Perennial, 2009), 330.

3   Karr, *The Art of Memoir* (New York: Harper Perennial, 2016).

4   Flannery O'Connor, quoted in John Adams, "Does Art Have to Be Relevant? One Prominent Critic Says No," *New York Times*, January 12, 2022.

5   Alain de Botton, *The School of Life: An Emotional Education* (London, UK: The School of Life, 2019).

6   Robert Farrar Capon, *Kingdom, Grace, Judgment: Paradox, Outrage, and Vindication in the Parables of Jesus* (Grand Rapids, MI: Eerdmans, 2002).

7   *Bohemian Rhapsody*, directed by Bryan Singer and Dexter Fletcher (2018; Los Angeles, CA: 20th Century Studios).

8   Mike Yaconelli, *Messy Spirituality: God's Annoying Love for Imperfect People* (Grand Rapids, MI: Zondervan, 2007), 65.

9   Capon, *The Romance of the Word: One Man's Love Affair with Theology* (Grand Rapids, MI: Eerdmans, 1996).

10 Walker Percy, *The Moviegoer* (New York: Farrar, Straus, and Giroux, 2019).

11 Aristotle, Quoted in Gerald G. May, *Addiction and Grace: Love and Spirituality in the Healing of Addictions* (New York: HarperOne, 2007), Annotated edition.

12 Augustine, *The Confessions of Saint Augustine* (New York: Penguin Classics, 1961).

13 Blaise Pascal, *Pensées* (London, UK: Penguin Classics, 1995).

14 Pascal, *Pensées.*

15 Brennan Manning, *The Ragamuffin Gospel: Good News for the Bedraggled, Beat-Up, and Burnt Out* (Colorado Springs, CO: Multnomah, 2005).

16 Manning, *All Is Grace: A Ragamuffin Memoir* (Colorado Springs, CO: David C. Cook Publishing, 2015).

17 Francis Spufford, *Unapologetic: Why, Despite Everything, Christianity Can Still Make Surprising Emotional Sense* (London, UK: Faber & Faber, 2013).

18 Brennan Manning and Greg Garrett, *The Prodigal: A Ragamuffin Story* (Grand Rapids, MI: Zondervan, 2013).

19 Eugene Peterson, *A Long Obedience in the Same Direction: Discipleship in an Instant Society* (Westmont, IL: InterVarsity Press, 1980).

20 Will Campbell, *Brother to a Dragonfly* (Jackson, MS: University Press of Mississippi, 2018).

21 Pat Conroy, "Anatomy of a Divorce," *Atlanta Magazine*, November 1, 1978.

22 Winn Collier, *A Burning in My Bones: The Authorized Biography of Eugene H. Peterson* (Colorado Springs, CO: WaterBrook, 2021).

23 Dwight Garner, "The Tracks of an Author's and a Reader's Tears," *The New York Times*, March 27, 2012, https://www.nytimes.com/2012/03/28/books/wild-by-cheryl-strayed-a-walkabout-of-reinvention.html.

24 Cheryl Strayed, *Tiny Beautiful Things: Advice from Dear Sugar* (New York: Knopf Doubleday, 2012).

25 Kathleen Norris, *Amazing Grace: A Vocabulary of Faith* (New York: Riverhead, Books 1999).

26 Norris, *Amazing Grace.*

27 Norris, *Amazing Grace.*

28 Paul Zahl, *Grace in Practice: A Theology of Everyday Life* (Grand Rapids, MI: Eerdmans, 2007).

29 John O'Donohue, "The Inner Landscape of Beauty," interview by Krista Tippett, *On Being with Krista Tippett* (blog), February 28, 2008.

30 William Hale White, *The Auto-Biography of Mark Rutherford* (Glasgow, UK: Good Press, 2021).

31 Conroy, "Anatomy of a Divorce."

32 Wendell Berry, *Sex, Economy, Freedom & Community* (New York: Pantheon, 1993).

33 Tchividjian, *Jesus + Nothing = Everything* (Denver, CO: FaithHappenings.com, 2020).

34 Mark Manson, *The Subtle Art of Not Giving a F*ck: A Counterintuitive Approach to Living a Good Life*, 2nd ed. (New York: Harper, 2016).

35 Sue Monk Kidd, *The Dance of the Dissident Daughter: A Woman's Journey from Christian Tradition to the Sacred Feminine* (San Francisco: Harper SanFrancisco, 1996).

36 "Ricky Garard Comes Clean," CrossFit Games Podcast Ep. 006, September 29, 2021.

37 Capon, *Between Noon and Three: Romance, Law, and the Outrage of Grace* (Grand Rapids, MI: Eerdmans, 1997), 232.

38 Capon, *The Romance of the Word: One Man's Love Affair with Theology* (Grand Rapids, MI: Eerdmans, 1996), 10.

39 Frederick Buechner, *Wishful Thinking: A Seeker's ABC* (San Francisco: HarperOne, 1993).

40 John Updike, *A Month of Sundays: A Novel* (New York: Random House, 1996).

41 Anne Lamott, *Bird by Bird: Some Instructions on Writing and Life* (New York: Knopf, 1995).

42 Nadia Bolz-Weber, "Stories of a Pro-*Choice* Christian," The Corners by Nadia Bolz-Weber (blog), June 30, 2022.

43 George N. Niederauer, "Flannery O'Connor's Religious Vision," *America – The Jesuit Review*, December 24, 2007.

44 Philip Yancey, *What's So Amazing About Grace?* (Grand Rapids, MI: Zondervan, 1997).

45 Jon Krakauer, *Into Thin Air: A Personal Account of the Mt. Everest Disaster* (New York: Anchor, 1999).

46 Berry, "Dismemberment," in *How It Went: Thirteen More Stories of the Port William Membership* (Berkeley, CA: Counterpoint, 2022), 68.

47 Berry, "Dismemberment," 73.

48 Berry, "Dismemberment," 74.

49 Berry, "Dismemberment," 77.

50 William Inge, *My Son Is a Splendid Driver* (Boston: Little, Brown and Company, 1971).

51 Inge, 152–153.

52 Rich Mullins, "The Love of God," released September 15, 1989, Reunion Records.

53 Berry, "Dismemberment," 77.

54 C. S. Lewis, from a letter to Mary Neylan, January 20, 1942.

55 Patricia Deegan, "Recovery: The Lived Experience of Rehabilitation," *Psychosocial Rehabilitation Journal*, 11, no. 4 (1988): 11–19.

56 Jane Kristen Marczewski, "God is on the Bathroom Floor," Nightbirde (blog), November 9, 2021.

57 Nick Cave and Sean O'Hagan, *Faith, Hope and Carnage* (New York: Farrar, Straus and Giroux, 2022).

58 David James Duncan, *God Laughs and Plays: Churchless Sermons in Response to the Preachments of the Fundamental Right* (Triad Institute, 2007).

59 Duncan, *God Laughs and Plays*.

60 Buechner, Buechner, Frederick. Story. In *Wishful Thinking: A Theological ABC*. Collins, 1973.

61 Andre Dubus III, *Townie: A Memoir* (New York: W. W. Norton & Co., 2012).

ABOUT THE AUTHOR

Tullian Tchividjian has authored numerous bestselling books and has traveled the world speaking about the healing power of grace. A grandson of Evangelist Billy Graham, Tullian spent years leading a famous megachurch before he crashed and burned in 2015.

In 2020, he and his wife Stacie founded The Sanctuary, a recovery place masquerading as a church in Jupiter, Florida. They have a blended family of five grown children and three grandchildren.

You can find him on social media here:

IG: @tulliantch
Facebook: @TullianT

www.ingramcontent.com/pod-product-compliance
Lightning Source LLC
Chambersburg PA
CBHW070036100426
42740CB00013B/2707